University of Nottingham

DEPARTMENT OF ADULT EDUCATION
(Joint Adult Classes Committee)

CIRCULATING LIBRARY

DATE DUE FOR RETURN

The loan period may be shortened if the item is requested.

THE FAMILY ECONOMY OF THE WORKING CLASSES IN THE COTTON INDUSTRY

THE
FAMILY ECONOMY OF THE WORKING CLASSES
IN THE COTTON INDUSTRY
1784–1833

by

FRANCES COLLIER

edited by
R. S. FITTON

MANCHESTER UNIVERSITY PRESS

© 1964 Manchester University Press

Published by the University of Manchester at the
UNIVERSITY PRESS
316–324 Oxford Road
Manchester, 13

First published 1964
Reprinted 1968

GB SBN 7190 0018 1

Printed in Great Britain by Butler & Tanner Ltd., Frome and London

FRANCES COLLIER

1889–1962

A Memoir by T. S. Ashton

It was by an unusual path that Frances Collier came to the University. Her father was a Manchester merchant who gave to music and literature at least as much of his energies as he gave to business. A friend of Adolph Brodsky and other leaders of musical life in the city, he was aware of the need for expert guidance to sharpen and discipline inborn aptitudes. One of his daughters was sent to study music at Leipzig; his son was given the training that enabled him to become a distinguished amateur 'cellist and a member of the Hallé Orchestra; and Fannie herself was taught to play the viola, so as to take her part in the family quartet. But of schooling, in the general sense of the word, Mr. Collier took a poor view: if the root of the matter was in you, you were best without the ministration of teachers. And so, apart from a short spell at a Dame School, Fannie was left to develop her intellectual interests alone, in a well-stocked library at home. In this case, at least, *laissez-faire* was vindicated. Her reading was both varied and close. There was, of course, Jane Austen, who remained a lifelong delight; but the two sterner authors who most deeply affected her mind as a girl were Marcus Aurelius, who reinforced the courage and altruism that were at the core of her being, and John Stuart Mill, who aroused a passionate concern for individual freedom and the emancipation of women.

At the age of sixteen or seventeen she joined the militant section of the Suffrage movement —the Women's Social and Political Union—and, though her only adventure was a chase by hooligans down one of the side-streets to Piccadilly, she saw a good deal of the heroism— and something of the petty rivalries—of its leading figures. At an early stage she began to ask herself seriously what might be the practical outcome of the winning of the vote. She had often heard it said that equality for women in politics would bring equality for them in earnings; but no one could tell her how exactly this would come about. When, in 1907, she put the question to an experienced politician he told her she could find the answer only by a study of Political Economy, and that for this she must go to the University. Her response was immediate. Professor S. J. Chapman and H. O. Meredith, amused but impressed by her eagerness, willingly admitted her to their classes, though without matriculation there could be no question of her reading for a degree.

During the following three years she enjoyed university life to the full. Most of her time was given to lectures and classes in Political Economy, Political Philosophy, Economic History and kindred subjects; but she also played an active part in the Economics Society, the Sociological Society, and other student bodies, in a circle the women members of which included Ellen Wilkinson, Susan Fairhurst and Maud Smith (afterwards Lady Woolton). An important event in her life, as in that of many others, was the coming to Manchester of George Unwin, under whose magnetic influence her chief interest turned from Marshallian economics to economic history. Unwin suggested that she should investigate some problems of a recent period; but she had already developed an interest in the effects of economic changes on the lives of the workers in the early cotton industry, and insisted on going her own way, with little more than nominal supervision. Most of her work on printed materials was done at Chetham's Hospital and the Central Reference Library—then under the control of a scholarly and generous man who, against all precedent, allowed her to take the Blue Books home. Progress was slow, for she now had to earn a living. Before the outbreak of war she was acting as Assistant Secretary of the Free Trade Union, and after 1914 was at work in her father's office, where she gained a knowledge of business methods that was to be of value in her later career. The death of a married sister, in the epidemic of 1918, left her with a family of young things to care for; and a little later she had to help to nurse her father through a long illness and, after his death, to look after her mother. It was in the midst of such domestic preoccupations that the thesis was completed and presented in 1921, under an Ordinance that allowed of the conferment of the degree of M.A. on students of special distinction who had not previously graduated.

In the same year Miss Collier became a member of the University staff. She had already helped G. W. Daniels to collect material for his book on *The Early English Cotton Industry* (1920), and her appointment to a post entitled 'Research Assistant in the Faculty of Commerce' seemed to promise further travels in related fields. In fact, it brought research to an end. For the number of students of economics and commerce was expanding rapidly, and most of the detailed administrative work fell to her. During the following thirty years the department continued to grow: the staff was enlarged; innovations were made in both the curriculum and methods of teaching; professors came and went. But, throughout, she saw to it that the essential traditions were preserved. The titles she held (Tutor to the Faculty, 1927–1950; Supervisor of Students of Social Administration, 1937–1946; Secretary of the Faculty, 1939–1945; Reader in Social Administration, 1946–1952) give only a faint indication of her functions. She dealt with the varied problems of students, encouraging those the Americans call 'fortunate deviates', but giving most of her time to the others who found the going hard. She established good relations with leading Manchester businesses and acted as an employment bureau for graduates. She composed differences between temperamental senior colleagues and settled weighty matters of policy over the innumerable cups of coffee and tea she made in her room. In the early days she had something to do with the influx to both evening and day classes of men and women engaged in local government, and later helped with the transformation of the Faculty of Commerce and Administration into one of Economic and Social Studies.

Her outstanding service, however, was the creation, in the 'thirties, of a Department of Social Administration. There was, at this time, an urgent need for more and better welfare workers (personnel managers as, regrettably, they came to be called), hospital almoners, housing managers, probation officers, and others concerned with mental health, child care, and family guidance. But Miss Collier's enthusiasm for Social Administration sprang less, perhaps, from her concern for social betterment—strong as this was—than from the prospect offered of new professional openings for women. The greater part of the teaching was left to specialists; but central to the course was her own set of twenty lectures on Social Economics, which many students found to be the most stimulating of those given in the Faculty. Her chief teaching, however, was given informally in conversation. There must be hundreds of women in professional posts today who recall such scraps of commonsense advice she gave them when they left the University as 'Remember to ask yourself each night, "How would you have liked to work for me today?" '. It was a question that surely she had never cause to put to herself.

Failing health compelled retirement in 1952. She spent the last ten years of her life, happily, with a friend from childhood, in a charming cottage at Charlbury in Oxfordshire—a place that became a resort for former students and colleagues in need of refreshment of spirit. Concerned with the troubles of others, she hid, or mocked at, her own. Her devotion to the University never flagged. She died suddenly, as she would have wished, on September 28, 1962.

Parts of the thesis have appeared in *Economic History*, Vol. II, No. 5 (1930), *The Manchester School*, Vol. VII, Nos. 1 and 2 (1936), and the *Memoirs and Proceedings of the Manchester Literary and Philosophical Society*, Vol. LXXXV (1941–1943). But continued requests to borrow the sole remaining copy led to the decision to publish the document in full. It is to be read as the work of a young scholar, written nearly forty-five years ago—well before the controversy between Hammond and Clapham about the effects of the industrial revolution on the lives of wage-earners. It shows how, during the period, there took place in the cotton industry a substitution of adult for child labour, and a reversal of the roles played by women and men. It provides information about family earnings and expenditure such as does not exist for any other body of workers at this time. And it throws a less lurid light on the condition of the child apprentices than had been afforded by earlier writers. As the thesis was nearing completion in 1921 a mass of manuscripts relating to Samuel Oldknow's mill at Mellor was deposited with the University, and, as a supplement to her work, Miss Collier wrote a few pages treating of the children employed here. Unfortunately no copy of these can now be traced. But a summary of her findings is given in George Unwin's *Samuel Oldknow and the Arkwrights* (p. 174). On a visit to Mellor she had had the good fortune to meet a lady, eighty years of age, whose mother had been brought from Chelsea, by stage-coach, to work as a child apprentice for Oldknow. When mention was made of the deplorable conditions of children in the early factories the response was an indignant protest. The old lady repeated accounts she had had from her mother of the abundant food, including meat and fruit, supplied to the apprentices at Mellor; of the games the children had played, after a long day's work, in the meadow that lay between the mill and the 'prentice house; of the procession, two by two, every Sunday morning and evening up the steep bank to Marple Church; and of the occasional holidays and treats provided by the employer. Memories are fallible: perhaps the hardships had been forgotten. But it is something to know that, here at least, the first phase of factory life had left no tradition of resentment. (As she was leaving, Miss Collier remarked inquiringly, 'You never married, Miss —?' 'No', was the reply, 'I shall live and die an old maid, like my mother before me'.)

Those concerned with the publication of this book were fortunate indeed to enlist the help of Dr. R. S. Fitton whose knowledge of the early cotton factories is unrivalled. Dr. Fitton has given much of his leisure for several months to the exacting tasks of tracing the sources used by Miss Collier, checking the accuracy of the statistics, correcting minor errors, and adding a number of notes, together with the statistical material in Appendices C, D, and E. He can be assured of deep gratitude. Generally, however, the thesis remains as originally written. Miss Collier always protested that her work was not worthy of publication; but the news, a few months before she died, that preparations for printing were under way gave her a modest satisfaction. The book will be treasured by many not only as a revealing study, but as a reminder of a vital personality: a courageous, wise, large-hearted, and very gentle woman.

T.S.A.

CONTENTS

LIST OF TABLES IN THE TEXT

(The titles of tables in Appendix B are given at the beginning of the appendix)

CHAPTER I

INTRODUCTION

i

IN THE following pages an attempt is made to throw some light on the position of families whose incomes were wholly or mainly derived from the cotton industry in certain parts of Lancashire and Cheshire during the period from the end of the eighteenth to the middle of the nineteenth century.

In this kind of study there are several difficulties, the greatest of which is the lack of suitable records. It has not been possible to present a continuous account of any group of workpeople in one place and in order to help to overcome this difficulty material has been collected relating to groups of cotton workers in places and during years which may be regarded as typical.

Information is widely scattered in the Reports of Parliamentary Committees and Commissions, in newspapers and pamphlets, in the writings of advocates and opponents of various reforms and of critics and defenders of the factory system. Fortunately, three new sources of information have recently become available. These consist of two wage books included among the material deposited at the University by McConnel and Company; a wage book at Chetham's Library belonging to Peel, Yates and Peel of Bury; a valuable set of records of Greg & Sons of Styal.

It is from these sources that facts have been collected concerning the social and economic position of working-class families. The bulk of the available printed material relates to times of distress (of which there were many in the period under consideration) and most attention was focused upon those sections that were in the worst circumstances. The result is that, so far as the majority of the cotton workers are concerned, a great deal has to be left to the imagination. There are many deficiencies in this survey, but one may hope that further research will bring to light other material and thus enable a more complete picture to be presented.

When we consider the family economy of the workpeople employed in the cotton industry, the three main phases in its technical development—the time before the introduction of machinery, the years when water was the chief source of power, and the period when steam power became predominant—also form well-marked periods in the social history of the workpeople and their families.

The most important reactions were those due to alterations in the type of labour demanded in the different processes, and the expansion of the industry in places where the local labour supply was scanty. The earliest inventions had the most disturbing effect upon the family life of the cotton workers, for much of the labour in the earliest mills consisted of apprentices who were separated from their families throughout the whole period of their apprenticeship. Generally speaking this phase of the factory system was of short duration and was succeeded by a demand for labour which could be supplied without breaking up family life.

ii

In the period before the introduction of machinery the cotton manufacture was carried on in the houses of the workpeople. It provided employment for all members of the family: spinning and its preparatory processes were performed by the women and children and weaving by the men. At this stage of its development the cotton industry was widely scattered over Lancashire and the adjacent parts of Cheshire, Derbyshire and Yorkshire. For our purpose it is hardly necessary to consider the way in which the manufacture was organized before the introduction of large-scale production. It is sufficient to say that the work was performed by the labour of the family, the weaver being responsible for all the processes in the manufacture. Where the family had insufficient labour, which was no doubt a common occurrence, the preparatory and spinning processes were done outside the family.[1] If the weaver was responsible for all the processes he, of course, had to pay for these operations, and the difference between these payments and what he received for the cloth constituted the earnings of himself and his family.

There are several well-known accounts of the textile industry in its domestic phase. Perhaps the best is that in which Defoe describes the woollen manufacturing district between Rochdale and Halifax.[2] Woollen cloth was being made and finished in almost every house he passed. The 'Women and Children carding, or spinning; all employed from the youngest to the oldest, scarce anything above four Years old, but its Hands were sufficient for its own Support', the men weaving, dyeing and dressing cloth. Perhaps the cotton manufacturing districts of Lancashire would not present so picturesque a sight because the finishing processes were mainly concentrated round London in the early years of the eighteenth century and 'lusty Fellows' would not have been seen at the dye vats. Apart from this difference, however, Defoe's description would probably apply to many of the houses in the villages and small towns in which the making of fustians and checks were the staple industry.

Samuel Crompton's eldest son, George, left an interesting account of the kind of work performed by the members of weavers' families who were able to support themselves at the age of four:

> I recollect that soon after I was able to walk I was employed in the cotton manufacture. My mother used to bat the cotton wool on a wire riddle. It was then put into a deep brown mug with a strong ley of soap suds. My mother then tucked up my petticoats about my waist, and put me into the tub to tread upon the cotton at the bottom. When a second riddleful was batted I was lifted out, it was placed in the mug, and I again trode it down. This process was continued until the mug became so full that I could no longer safely stand in it, when a chair was placed besides it, and I held on by the back. When the mug was quite full, the soap suds were poured off, and each separate *dollop* of wool well squeezed to free it from moisture. They were then placed on the bread-rack under the beams of the kitchen-loft to dry. My mother and my grandmother carded the cotton wool by hand, taking one of the *dollops* at a time, on the simple hand-cards. When carded they were put aside in separate parcels ready for spinning.[3]

[1] G. W. Daniels, *The Early English Cotton Industry*, Manchester, 1920, p. 37. It was not unusual for weavers to obtain apprentices from parish apprentices (evidence of Dr. Kinder Wood of Oldham, *Minutes of Evidence taken before the Select Committee of the Children employed in the Manufactories of the United Kingdom*, 1816, p. 205).

[2] Daniel Defoe, *A Tour Thro' the Whole Island of Great Britain*, Vol. III, London, 1738, pp. 78–9.

[3] Gilbert J. French, *The Life and Times of Samuel Crompton*, third edition, Manchester, 1862, pp. 58–9.

Another description of a family engaged in the cotton manufacture in the 1760s and 1770s is given by William Radcliffe:[1]

> The principal estates being gone from the family, my father resorted to the common but never-failing resource for subsistence at that period, VIZ.—the loom for men, and the cards and hand-wheel for women and boys. He married a spinster, (in my etymology of the word) and my mother taught me (while too young to weave) to earn my bread by carding and spinning cotton, winding linen or cotton weft for my father and elder brothers at the loom, until I became of sufficient age and strength for my father to put me into a loom.

The second period begins with the success of Arkwright's experiments which took spinning and many of the preparatory processes out of the home into the factory. The labour demanded by the new processes was of the same type as before, the new machinery being adapted for the employment of women and children. The changes involved arose owing to the great demand for labour at certain places whereas previously the workpeople had been scattered throughout the cotton manufacturing area. Consequently, even had there been no prejudice against entering the factories it would have been impossible for most of the people who had worked in their own homes to become millhands. To do so would have involved migration and as the early spinning mills absorbed little skilled male labour there was no great attraction for weaving families to move. Hence many of the factory masters resorted to the apprenticeship system and much of the male labour which migrated to factory towns was unskilled, or had families for whom employment in a cotton mill meant a substantial increase of income.

As the weavers' families lost their work of preparing and spinning cotton, the men lost their monopoly of weaving. Indeed, between the two events there was a close connection for, by seeking employment at the looms for those members of their families who had previously prepared their yarn, the weavers hastened a development which was inevitable since it was found that neither a man's strength nor much skill were required to weave the new cloths. From the 1790s onwards women, boys and girls were employed in ever-increasing numbers in weaving calicoes, coarse muslins and cambrics.

The third phase starts with the introduction of steam power, the invention of the mule, and the growth of the cotton industry in towns.[2] With the expansion of mule spinning and the improvement of the machinery used in the manufacture the need for skilled male labour increased and the abnormal demand for child labour diminished. At the close of our period, with the exception of male handloom weavers who were in a parlous position, the industry as a whole had returned to a more healthy condition, providing employment, if not for full proportions of men to women and children, at least for more adult than juvenile labour. Machinery had reversed the occupations of the sexes—women had attained the predominance they still have in the weaving, and men in the spinning branch of the industry.

Our records relate to several types of firms which belong to the different stages of factory development. The material enables us to give some account of the kinds of labour employed and the conditions under which the workers lived, as well as to form some idea of the social and economic position of the families to which they belonged.

---

[1] William Radcliffe, *Origin of the New System of Manufacture, commonly called 'Power-Loom Weaving'*, Stockport, 1828, pp. 9–10.

[2] There is, of course, no rigid line of demarcation between the two periods of factory development but it is well known that after the introduction of steam power the factory industry tended to concentrate in towns and mule spinning became predominant.

CHAPTER II

ECONOMIC AND POLITICAL BACKGROUND

THE SPINNERS

THE great expansion of the cotton industry which followed the introduction of the factory system took place during the Napoleonic Wars and an already difficult situation was made immensely more complex owing to the great fluctuations of trade for which war conditions, and the aftermath of war, were largely responsible. The short periods of boom, when capital and labour were attracted to the rapidly growing industry were followed by long periods of depression and slow recovery, when only the most efficient firms expanded, and when workers in both the spinning and weaving branches of the industry suffered from the misfortunes which overtook their trade.

Whatever the disadvantages of the factory system, there can be no question as to the better position of the factory workers in times of depression compared with those still employed outside the factory. The strength of the factory operatives and the weakness of the handloom weavers is clearly revealed in the course of their wages and employment, long before the weavers were competing with new machinery to any extent.

From the beginning of the factory system in the cotton industry, the wages of the operatives were relatively high as compared with those which the same type of labour could have obtained in other occupations. As machinery was improved the industry expanded, the number of people employed in factories became greater, and the proportion of well-paid jobs increased. Throughout the period, during which the cotton trade experienced a vicissitude of fortunes, the rates of wages of the factory workers fluctuated much less than did those of weavers.

This does not mean that the factory operatives altogether escaped the hard times. They suffered from unemployment or, more usually, underemployment, and in times of depression they were forced to submit to reductions in their rates of wages. But, so far as the majority of them was concerned, these reductions took place very occasionally and then only for small amounts. Apart from the years of commercial disaster, and cases where changes in processes involved an alteration in the kind of labour employed, the wages of workers in the preparatory processes of spinning remained almost stationary.

Adult male mule spinners, a small and highly skilled class,[1] suffered more frequently from reductions than did other operatives and when the reduction was general their wages fell by a greater amount than those of any other section of workpeople.[2] Furthermore over

---

[1] The average weekly net earnings of the 111 spinners employed at Thomas Houldsworth's Manchester mill came to 33s. 6d. in 1833 as compared with the 7s. 1d. of the 913 persons engaged in carding, doubling, reeling and piecing (*Select Committee on Manufactures, Commerce, and Shipping*, 1833, p. 320).

[2] During the distress of 1839 Stockport spinners had their wages reduced 30 per cent, carders 7½ per cent and weavers 9–10 per cent. 'Apart from the short time worked, there has been a reduction of wages in Stockport within the last two years', stated Mr. M'Clure, manager of Orrel's cotton mill (*Report . . . into the State of the Population of Stockport*, 1842, p. 44).

a period of years their piece rates declined, but only as improvements in machinery enabled greater quantities of yarn to be turned out. This may be illustrated by the figures from the wage-books of Thomas Houldsworth of Manchester (Table I):[1]

TABLE I

DECLINE IN PIECE RATES

Year	No. of Counts	Work done by one spinner (lb. per week)	Wages (Net)	No. of Counts	Work done by one spinner (lb. per week)	Wages (Net)
1804	180	12	32s. 6d.	200	9	36s. 6d.
1814	180	18	44s. 6d.	200	13½	60s. 0d.
1833	180	22½	33s. 8d.	200	19	42s. 9d.

Houldsworth's spinners were able to maintain their piece rates and obtain benefit from the increased output until after the Napoleonic Wars when rates were reduced. By 1833 the fine spinners were turning out 10½ lb. of 180 counts above the quantity spun in 1804, while their earnings came to only 1s. 2d. more. McConnel and Kennedy had reduced their piece rates in November, 1810, and it seems that other spinners did so before the end of hostilities.

Several reasons may be suggested for this tendency for wage-rates to be maintained in the face of the great changes which occurred in the industry. In the first place the employers had a large amount of capital invested in buildings and machinery and this induced them to keep their factories running until they reached the point at which they failed to meet prime costs. There was also great scope for gaining economies in the factories and the desire to reduce the costs of production in order to expand the market by offering cheaper yarn led to more efficient organization. Further, the profits of the master spinners in the early days of the factory industry were so large that their numbers rapidly increased and, owing to this competition, profits had to bear a large proportion of the fall in prices.

There are no statistics relating to this diminution of profits during the Napoleonic Wars, but the fact is illustrated by Appendix B, Table I, compiled by George Smith, partner in James Massey and Son, cotton spinners and handloom calico manufacturers of Manchester, a concern employing 1,300–1,400 workpeople.

Smith stated that while the price obtained for the yarn steadily declined 'there may have been some slight reduction in the price of spinning' during the ten to twelve years ending in 1833.[2] As the amount left for labour, expenses and profit was 72 per cent less in 1832 than in 1815 it is clear that profits, which had been extremely high in 1815, must have been extremely low in 1832. It is equally clear that earnings were not such as would allow of any substantial portion of the decline being shifted on to them. Smith's evidence referred to coarse yarns for which the cost of labour was proportionately less than in the production in fine yarns, but the complaints of other master spinners indicate that much the same process was taking place in fine mule spinning.

But although it would have been impossible for the workers to bear much of the decline,

[1] *Select Committee on Manufactures, Commerce, and Shipping*, 1833, p. 319.
[2] *Ibid.*, p. 551.

the fact that their earnings were so little affected was, no doubt, largely influenced by the vigorous way in which they resisted any attempt to lower their wages, and by their power to bring the mills to a standstill.

THE HANDLOOM WEAVERS

When we turn to the handloom weavers, who constituted much the larger body of cotton workers, we find that the factors which tended to stabilize the position of the millhands were absent.

The first great source of weakness in their position was the small amount of fixed capital employed in the manufacture of cloth. The processes of manufacture were usually carried on in the homes of the workpeople and the machinery and tools required were inexpensive. Hence the principal part of the employer's capital was invested in the materials he gave out to the weavers (unless he was in business in a big way and held large stocks of cloth) and a small outlay enabled a man with little capital to embark on the career of a manufacturer—as many did.

Probably these men were instrumental in extending the industry but, according to the accusations of the weavers, their conduct in times of stress did not help to steady markets. No doubt the accusations were well-founded, for, as the manufacturers usually possessed little or no reserve, they were the first in slack times to reduce prices in order to dispose of their cloth. As the heralds of approaching distress they were frequently attributed with the responsibility for causing it.

It was through these men, however, that in brisk times there arose a very great demand for weavers. If a man had a room and could rent a loom, or had 40s. with which to buy one, he could become a weaver; and because of the facility with which newcomers acquired the necessary skill to weave the staple cloths, people who came to the cotton centres drifted into an occupation in which it was easy to eke out a living. Many families included more than one weaver, for women and young persons could weave the lower qualities of cloth, and by the beginning of the nineteenth century the ranks of the weavers contained all sorts and conditions of men, women and children.[1]

Under conditions such as these, in an industry which was constantly undergoing modification, and with no greater weapon than the refusal of work—which at most caused their employers to lose some trade—it is not difficult to realize why the handloom weavers as a class were doomed to a progressive deterioration of standards.

It must be borne in mind, however, that although all sections of the weavers suffered a diminution of income many of them were earning but a modest sum to begin with. The weavers in all branches of the manufacture did not experience a descent from great prosperity to adversity. At no period does it appear that high prices were common for the weaving of fustians, checks, and smallwares, and it is also doubtful whether those engaged upon the calicoes and coarse cotton cloths, manufactured after the water-frame was introduced, ever received the high wages paid to the weavers of muslins and cambrics. It was the first generation of this class of weavers, whose product was a novelty which brought fancy prices when

---

[1] In 1804 the weavers of Bolton (the centre for cambrics) presented a petition praying Parliament to fix a rate of wages upon the principle of the Spitalfields Act (*Select Committee on Manufactures, Commerce, and Shipping*, 1833, p. 705).

first put on the market, that enjoyed a spell of very high wages.[1] Even then the time of prosperity cannot have been a very long one, for although in 1780 Crompton perfected his mule which made possible the manufacture of fine cotton cloths, some years elapsed before it became in general use; and by 1797 the decline had begun which, with several fluctuations, culminated in the displacement of the hand loom and the acute distress of those weavers who continued to cling to their occupation.

The first fall in the price of cotton cloth was the natural result of the greatly increased supply; then came the troublous times during the Napoleonic conflict, which were in turn outmatched by the depression which came with peace. The cost of the raw materials fell with the general fall in prices, but the prices obtained for cloth fell considerably faster and, as is shown in Appendix B, Table II, nearly all the decline had to be borne by labour. During the war profits had varied but on the whole they had been cut so fine that there was no margin to fall back upon as in the case of the spinners.

In any circumstances the manufacturers would not have risked as much as the spinners. Motives of humanity may have prompted some of them to continue giving out work for a time but it was not to their interest to manufacture cloth in a falling market, at a cost which they could see no prospect of covering, when they could reduce or put an end to their losses by waiting. Consequently large numbers of weavers were thrown out of employment and had to resort to charity until such times as they could obtain work.

Perhaps sufficient has been said to indicate the general causes of the marked contrast between the economic position of the families of handloom weavers and those of the factory hands. The latter had a chance of improving their standard of living while the handloom weavers were compelled to lower their's until they were living in destitution. The two classes were not, of course, rigidly divided, for many weavers living in the neighbourhood of factories relieved their situation by sending their children to work in them. The greatest suffering was endured in those districts where no employment but weaving could be obtained and children had to be brought up to their parents' occupation. By the time the distress of the weavers had roused the Government to undertake an enquiry into its causes[2] the power loom was capable of producing all the standard cloths and the position of the handloom weavers was beyond remedy. In places where there was an opportunity of other employment, only those lacking initiative lingered on in the industry.

THE STATE OF TRADE

The position of the handloom weavers, as of others engaged in the cotton industry, was, of course, dependent upon the state of trade. It is advisable, therefore, before passing to a more detailed study of the life of the cotton workers, to glance at the principal landmarks in the eventful half-century which followed the establishment of cotton as a factory industry.

Until 1833 the statistics relating to the development of the industry are confined to the official returns of the amount of raw cotton and manufactured goods imported into and exported from this country. These show an enormous increase in production (which involved

[1] The prices of weaving cambrics show a continuous decline during the period 1795–1833 set out in the table supplied by R. Needham and W. Pilling of Great Bolton (*Select Committee on Manufactures, Commerce, and Shipping, 1833* pp. 699–700).

[2] *Report of the Commissioners on the Hand-Loom Weavers*, 1841.

a great if not corresponding increase in the amount of labour employed) and an almost continuous decline in prices. Table II provides a setting of the progress of the industry in each decade from 1781 to the middle of the nineteenth century:[1]

TABLE II

PROGRESS OF THE COTTON INDUSTRY, 1781–1849

Year	Quantity of cotton wool taken for consumption (lb.)	Value of Goods Exported (£)	
		Official	Real or Declared
1781	5,198,778	(1780) 355,060	
1791	28,706,675	1,875,046	
1801	54,203,433	7,050,809	
1811	90,309,668	12,013,149	
1821	137,401,549	22,541,615	16,093,787
1831	273,249,653	39,357,075	17,257,204
1841	437,093,631	69,798,131	23,499,478
1849	775,469,008	112,416,294	26,771,432

The manufacture of goods in which cotton was used was, of course, an important Lancashire industry for long before the late eighteenth century. Goods made of a mixture of linen and cotton were manufactured probably in the sixteenth century and by the middle of the seventeenth century a wide range of goods was produced in which cotton was used.[2] With the introduction of roller-spinning in the 1770s the industry entered upon a new phase for which Arkwright and his partners were largely responsible.

The great increase in the amount of cotton imported after the loss and expiration of Arkwright's patent rights shows how quickly the manufacture grew; from 1783 to 1792 imports increased from 9,735,663 lb. to 34,907,497 lb.—a figure which was not reached again for seven years.[3] The check to the industry which the falling off in the import of cotton denotes was due to the outbreak of war with France. The opening of hostilities was marked by many bankruptcies and by widespread unemployment in the manufacturing centres.[4]

The industry did not recover from this shock until prospects of peace appeared at the end of the eighteenth century when an effort was made to meet the great demand for goods which was confidently expected once the political situation was settled. New mills were built, established concerns enlarged their works, and the highest hopes were entertained of the future of the industry.

The position was changed when war broke out again in May, 1803. Throughout the whole

[1] The returns for 1781–1791 are taken from E. Baines, *History of the Cotton Manufacture in Great Britain*, London, 1835, pp. 347, 349 and those for 1801–1849 from G. R. Porter, *The Progress of the Nation*, London, 1851, p. 178.

[2] G. W. Daniels, *The Early English Cotton Industry*, p. 25.

[3] Baines, *op. cit.*, p. 347. In 1799 43,379,278 lb. were imported.

[4] Information about the state of the cotton trade during these years has been obtained from G. W. Daniels's papers 'The Cotton Trade During the Revolutionary and Napoleonic Wars', *Trans. Manch. Stat. Soc.* (1915–1916) and 'The Cotton Trade at the Close of the Napoleonic War', *Trans. Manch. Stat. Soc.* (1917–1918).

of this second phase of the conflict with France conditions in the cotton trade were very unsettled, and during the closing years of the war, when restrictions were placed on commerce by France, Britain and the United States the outlook became hopeless.

The situation became critical early in 1807 when trade was so bad that large numbers of people were unemployed. Some factories closed down, and many went on to half-time. The American Embargo Act of December, 1807, worsened matters and brought an influx of petitions to Parliament. Petitions from Manchester and Bolton asked for peace negotiations to be opened and those from manufacturers and merchants of London, Manchester and Liverpool prayed for the repeal of the Orders in Council.[1] An enquiry was held into the operation of the Orders in 1808 but the evidence of the financial embarrassment of merchants and employers, and the distress of the working class led to nothing.

The winter of 1808–1809 was a severe one. 'There never was any period, perhaps in the history of Manchester, when the distresses of the poorer classes were greater than at the present juncture', recorded the *Manchester Mercury* of January 3, 1809. It went on to commend the people of Ardwick not only for making a generous subscription on behalf of the poor but also for distributing potatoes, clothing, blankets and coal to the needy.

In June, 1809, however, trade revived owing to a sudden export of goods to South America. The boom lasted just long enough for speculators to realize the extent of their folly; the exports brought few returns and in 1810 bankruptcies and distress signalized commercial collapse.

The next two years were the worst of the war. Trade was paralysed, money depreciated, and food was scarce. In 1811 the Luddites rioted in Nottingham and there were food riots in other manufacturing towns. The following year machine breaking extended to Lancashire, Cheshire and Yorkshire.[2] Although punishing the rioters with the utmost rigour of the law, the Government could no longer ignore the outcry from all connected with trade and industry and another enquiry was held which resulted in the revocation of the Orders in Council. Unhappily this came too late to avoid war with America.

A revival of trade came at the end of 1812 and continued into January, 1813, after which a decline appears to have taken place. But soon afterwards trade was being re-opened with the Continent, a plentiful harvest reduced food prices, and the military situation raised hopes that the end of the conflict was in sight.[3]

With the coming of peace heavy shipments of cotton goods were made to the Continent and by the close of 1814 the industry was entering upon another boom, the outcome of which is well described in the words of Brougham:

> The bubble soon burst, like its predecessors of the South Sea, Mississippi, and Buenos Ayres. English goods were selling for much less in Holland and the North of Europe, than in London and Manchester; in most places they were lying a dead-weight without any sale at all; and either no returns whatever were received, or pounds came back for thousands that had gone forth.[4]

1816 was a year of general distress. Credit was shaken, industry at a standstill, and food

---

[1] *Hansard*, February 22, 1808 (p. 693) and March 18, 1808 (p. 1182).
[2] G. W. Daniels, 'The Cotton Trade at the Close of the Napoleonic War', *Trans. Manch. Stat. Soc.* (1917–1918).
[3] *Annual Register*, 1813, p. 103.
[4] Harriet Martineau, *A History of England during The Thirty Years' Peace, 1816–1846*, London, 1877, Vol. I, p. 53.

at famine prices.[1] The cotton trade shared in the general depression. Spinning firms were evidently in difficulties, for the spinners were persuaded to agree to a reduction of wages on the understanding that the old rates would be restored when trade improved. The mills appear to have run full-time in spite of the bad trade, and the hardships endured by the workpeople were mainly due to high prices.[2] This was not the case with the weavers who were in a parlous state as manufacturers reduced their work to a minimum or stopped giving it out altogether; employment was considered a favour and wages sank lower and lower.[3]

The efforts to relieve the sufferings of the working classes could do little. Unrest was prevalent in all parts of the country. In the manufacturing towns of the north the people pinned their faith to Parliamentary reform as a remedy for the ills they were enduring and for the next two years caused the Government much anxiety by the prominent part they took in the agitation for a wider franchise.[4]

In 1818 Manchester spinners turned out for their old rates but the state of the market was against them. They met with strenuous resistance from their employers and after a prolonged struggle returned to work at the rates of 1816.

The political troubles of 1819 bear eloquent testimony to the widespread distress. Five years of low wages, unemployment and dear food created bitter resentment against the Government and its supporters but its public expression was checked for a time by the dispersion of the Peterloo meeting in August and by the prosecutions which followed it. Before the reformers had recovered from this blow it became clear that the situation that was winning them so many converts had altered for the better. During 1820 trade was slowly recovering and a plentiful harvest, the first of a series, reduced the price of food and put an end to acute distress.[5]

[1] In January the average price of wheat was 52s. 6d., in May 76s. 4d. and at the end of the year 103s. Rye, barley and beans more than doubled in price (Martineau, *op. cit.*, p. 61).

[2] According to George Gould, who presented twenty-two instances, Manchester factories were running 14–15 hours a day, including meal times (*Minutes of Evidence taken before the Select Committee of the Children employed in the Manufactories of the United Kingdom*, 1816, pp. 96–7).

[3] *Ibid.*, pp. 99–100.

[4] The close association between reform and food is illustrated by the following passage from a speech at a reform meeting in Manchester in 1816:

The only remedy for the accumulated ills which you now suffer, is in rallying round the Constitution, which the swords of our ancestors so gloriously won, and wresting from the Borough Faction your long lost rights, that of electing your own Representatives, and making the House of Commons to express the real voice of the people. . . . Lord Arden to be sure, will not receive 39,000 1-pound (*sic*) a year of your money, nor the long list of Placemen and extravagant Pensioners be rolling in luxury, on the produce of your labour, while you are starving but you and your families will be well fed and well clothed, smiling plenty will again resume her sway within your now miserable habitations, and England will again become, what it once was, and what it ought to be, 'A land of Roast Beef and Plum Pudding'—(*Shouts of applause*).

(*A Report of the Proceedings of the Public Meeting . . . near the Quaker's Chapel, Manchester, On Monday, Oct. 28th, 1816*, Manchester, 1816, p. 9; the pamphlet, No. 21,641, is in Chetham's Library, Manchester.) There 'having been many gross and wilful misrepresentations respecting the number of persons who attended this meeting', the organizers, after some tedious calculations, put the figure at above 51,000 (*ibid.*, p. 24). The *Manchester Mercury* (October 29, 1816) had reported: 'It is calculated that there were no more than five thousand people present, two thousand of whom could be only deemed actual participators in the transactions of the day—a very insignificant crowd'.

[5] The 'yearly average prices of Grain in England and Wales', 1815–1821, calculated from the weekly returns published in the *Gazette* and reprinted in the *Manchester Guardian*, November 24, 1821, are shown on the opposite page.

In 1821 the *Manchester Guardian* referred to the larger number of well-dressed working class people who were able to attend the Whit Week races owing to their 'present comfortable circumstances'.[1] Trade, however, was still far from prosperous; a committee of the Manchester Chamber of Commerce which examined thirty-one of the 'most intelligent and experienced' spinners and manufacturers of the town, reported that twenty-eight of the witnesses had not only carried on an unprofitable trade for years but had suffered severe losses and that many of them 'would gladly withdraw from it altogether, if it were not for the immense sacrifice which would attend the breaking up of their establishments'.[2] The newspaper summarized the position at the end of 1821 as follows:

> there is as little question that it [the cotton trade] has not, upon the average, for years past, afforded those engaged in it a due remuneration for their capital and exertions. . . . Ever since the peace, the prices of raw material, and of the manufactured goods, have been coming down; and it is, therefore, impossible that dealers in those articles should have been able to realize those regular profits, which, in a settled state of trade, they might fairly have looked to obtain.[3]

The years 1822 and 1823 were marked by steady progress. The transition from war to peace conditions now seemed complete and the outlook for the future most hopeful. Unfortunately, however, the industry was soon to experience another crisis followed by a long period of depression.

As in the mania of 1815, the speculation in cotton goods which began in 1824, was part of a general trade boom, although this time on a much larger scale. Money was plentiful and cheap[4] and under the prevailing spirit of optimism was invested in any project which seemed likely to realize profits. The objects of many of the companies that were floated were so foolish that the fact that they obtained support at all is some indication of the rush that took place to invest money in well-established industries. Capital poured into the cotton industry and a scramble started to build new mills and to enlarge old ones.

As early as the summer of 1824 the exchanges had turned against Britain and bullion was being exported. The inevitable collapse came late in the following year. In July the issues of the Bank of England began to be restricted and in November several country banks failed.[5] At the beginning of December two big London banks stopped payments[6] and in

Year Ending	Wheat	Rye	Barley	Oats	Beans	Peas
	s. d.	s. d.	s. d.	s. d.	s. d.	s. d.
October 28, 1815	66 6	39 0¼	31 6	24 5¼	37 9¾	40 8
October 26, 1816	72 4¾	40 11¼	32 3½	23 3½	36 3¼	36 8¼
October 25, 1817	97 6	58 9¼	49 0½	32 8	53 2	51 9¾
October 24, 1818	84 1¼	52 8	50 3¼	31 8¾	59 1¼	55 11½
October 30, 1819	75 0	52 7	51 7½	31 2	60 4	60 4
October 28, 1820	67 3¾	41 10¼	35 3¾	24 9½	44 10½	46 5½
November 2, 1821.	55 1	24 4	26 7	20 1	28 1	31 10

[1] June 16, 1821.

[2] *Manchester Guardian*, December 8, 1821.

[3] *Ibid.*, December 15, 1821.

[4] In 1825 the Bank of England lowered the rate of interest. There was at that time 30–40 per cent more paper money in circulation than in 1822 (Martineau, *op. cit.* Vol. II, p. 6.

[5] At this time 'Many a man set up for a banker who would, at another time, have as soon thought of setting up for a king' (*ibid.*, Vol. II, p. 5).

[6] Sir Peter Pole & Co. and Williams & Co. (*ibid.*, p. 13).

the course of a few weeks sixty or seventy other banks did the same and the collapse was complete.

The extensive failures of these country banks resulted in the bankruptcy of many drapers and ruined the home trade in cotton goods.[1] Large stocks, accumulated in the belief that prices would continue to rise, depreciated within a few weeks to half their value. The panic reached its height in January, 1826; it was checked when the Bank of England agreed to advance up to £3 million on merchants' goods but it was years before trade recovered from the gamble of 1824–1825.

1826 was a year of exceptional distress for the cotton workers. Funds were raised for their relief in the manufacturing towns and it is not surprising that this year witnessed the destruction of power looms by mobs of rioters.

The cotton industry recovered but slowly from this collapse. The boom had led to such an increase in the number of firms engaged in cotton spinning that the industry suffered from excess capacity. Trade increased in volume but only at lower prices and spinners were compelled to seek every means possible to reduce the costs of production. This was done chiefly by speeding-up machinery and by adding power-loom weaving to spinning. Yet even when these changes had been made profits were so low that no new mills were built in Manchester between 1825 and 1833 and there was little extension in outlying districts.[2] Such was the gist of the evidence given by spinners and manufacturers before the *Select Committee on Manufactures, Commerce, and Shipping*, but shortly after the enquiry was held industry showed signs of recovery.

In a report made by Dr. Kay to the Poor Law Commissioners in July, 1835, details are given of a big expansion that was taking place in the cotton industry. He estimated that £3,753,000 was being invested within two years in buildings and machinery which he calculated would involve a demand for 45,042 mill hands.[3] After examining the possible sources from which labour could be obtained in the districts in which this expansion was taking place he advised the Commissioners to encourage the migration of agricultural labouring families from the south of England as 'the only alternative to an extensive immigration of Irish' which he considered to be 'not an unmingled benefit'. But migration should proceed with great caution 'lest at any moment the supply outstrip the legitimate demand'.[4]

The circumstances which encouraged this development, and its outcome, were investigated by the Commissioners who enquired into the distress in Stockport in 1842. From returns they obtained it appears that 11,826 horse power (4,319 more than Dr. Kay had estimated as in course of erection or ordered) were erected in parts of Lancashire and Cheshire between January, 1835 and July, 1838.[5] According to the Commissioners the causes of this expansion were to be found in the extension of the home market due to the low price of cereals, which enabled the working classes to spend a larger proportion of their income on clothing, in the

---

[1] Archibald Prentice, *Historical Sketches and Personal Recollections of Manchester*, second edition, London and Manchester, 1851, p. 270.

[2] *Select Committee on Manufactures, Commerce, and Shipping*, 1833, pp. 554, 648, 651–3, 684.

[3] *First Annual Report of the Poor Law Commissioners for England and Wales*, 1835, p. 187.

[4] *Ibid.*, pp. 185, 188.

[5] *Evidence taken, and Report made, by the Assistant Poor Law Commissioners sent to inquire into the State of the Population of Stockport*, 1842, pp. 53–4.

ease with which loans could be obtained from joint-stock banks[1] and in the great demand for cotton goods in America.[2]

The autumn of 1836 witnessed a reversal of these favourable conditions and the inevitable consequences of rampant speculation. The trouble started with a financial panic in America which caused the failure of many houses in the American trade which had borrowed heavily from joint-stock banks to finance their businesses.[3] Later a run on these banks shook them to their foundations and although prompt action on the part of the Bank of England saved a repetition of the bank failures of 1825 the shock to public confidence, coupled with the pressure put on persons to whom the banks had advanced loans, led to a period of acute commercial distress. The finishing touch to the disaster, so far as the cotton trade was concerned, was the failure of the harvest which raised the price of food and cut down the home demand for cloth to a minimum.

This broad outline of the state of trade in the period under consideration shows that the growth of the industry was far from continuous. The important point is that when spells of good trade did come they lasted long enough to encourage expansion and that, when the booms were over, the industry adapted itself to the new conditions so that after each period of expansion a much larger number of people depended on the industry for their livelihood.

As might be expected some firms settled down to the new conditions with less trouble than others, and in generalizing about the factory workers this difference must be recognized, for it created a distinction of the same kind, but of a lesser degree, as that between factory workers as a class and the handloom weavers as a class. While some operatives in bad times underwent great hardships through the inability of their employers to cope with the situation, others, employed by more able men or by firms in a better position, suffered only a diminution of income not intensified by unemployment.

[1] *Evidence taken, and Report made, by the Assistant Poor Law Commissioners sent to inquire into the State of the Population of Stockport, 1842*, p. 55.

[2] *Ibid.*, p. 56.

[3] Six houses in London and one in Liverpool had made advances on American accounts to no less than £15 million while their means of meeting these liabilities were under one-sixth of the whole. Three suspended payment but were helped by the Bank of England in order to avoid the failure of the other houses (Martineau, *op. cit.*, Vol. III, p. 365).

CHAPTER III

McCONNEL AND KENNEDY'S MANCHESTER MILL

1795 AND 1810–1819

RECRUITMENT OF LABOUR IN TOWN AND COUNTRY

THE factory system first made its appearance not in the large towns where it later became concentrated, but in the country districts. In 1783 when two Scotsmen came to Manchester from Morayshire with a letter of recommendation from William Grant[1] to Richard Arkwright, through which they hoped to obtain employment at his mill, Manchester had two mills: Arkwright's in Piccadilly, which was on 'a small scale',[2] and Thackray's mill situated near Granby Row. Another letter, written by Grant's son more than half a century later, to an unnamed person who proposed to publish a book about the beginnings of the Lancashire cotton industry—an intention never realized—reads as follows:[3]

Springside, *May 17, 1839.*

Dear Sir,—Allow me to acknowledge the receipt of your esteemed favour of the 10th. My father was a dealer in cattle, and lost his property in the year 1783. He got a letter of introduction to Mr. Arkwright (the late Sir Richard) and came by way of Skipton and Manchester, accompanied by me. As we passed along the old road, we stopped for a short time on the Park estate to view the valley. My father exclaimed, 'What a beautiful valley! May God Almighty bless it!' It reminded me of Speyside, but the Irwell is not so large as the river Spey.

I recollected that Messrs. Peel & Yates were then laying the foundation of their printworks at Ramsbottom. We went forward to Manchester and called upon Mr. Arkwright, but he had so many applications then he could not employ him. There were then only Arkwright's mill, on a small scale, and Thacary's (*sic*) mill in Manchester. There was a mill on the Irwell belonging to Mr. Douglas, two belonging to Messrs. Peel & Yates, the one at Radcliffe Bridge the other at Hinds; and these were the only mills then in Lancashire. My father then applied to Mr. Dinwiddie, a Scotch gentleman, who knew him in his prosperity, and who was a printer and manufacturer at Hampson Mill, near Bury. He agreed to give my father employment, and placed my brother James and me in situations, where we had an opportunity of acquiring a knowledge both of manufacturing and printing; and offered me a partnership when I had finished my apprenticeship. I declined his offer, and commenced business for myself on a small scale, assisted by my brothers John, Daniel, and Charles, and removed to Bury, where I was very successful, and in the course of a few years (in 1800?) I removed to Manchester, and commenced printing in partnership with my brothers. My brother Daniel commenced travelling through the North of England and almost to every market town in Scotland. In 1806 we purchased the print works

---

[1] William Grant died at his residence, Grant Lodge, near Bury, on June 29, 1817, aged eighty-four. 'To the strictest integrity he added a truly benevolent mind, and a constant practice up to his latest moments of the moral duties incumbent on the christian' (*Manchester Mercury*, July 8, 1817).

[2] In 1782 Arkwright asserted that 5,000 persons were employed in factories built on his principle and that he and his partners had invested £30,000 in the construction and equipping of cotton mills (G. W. Daniels, *The Early English Cotton Industry*, p. 100).

[3] The letter is reproduced in W. Hume Elliot, *The Story of the 'Cheeryble' Grants*, Manchester and London, 1906, pp. 197–9.

belonging to Sir Robert Peel, &c., situated at Ramsbottom. In 1812 we purchased Nuttall factory. In consequence of the death of Mr. Alsop, the workpeople had been long short of employment, and were very destitute. We ordered the manager to get new machinery of the first-rate construction, and greatly extended the building; and before we began to spin or manufacture we clothed the whole of the hands at our own expense, prepared an entertainment for them, and observed that the interests of masters and servants are bound together, that there are reciprocal duties to perform, that no general or admiral could be brave unless he was supported by his men, that we knew how to reward merit, and would give constant employment and liberal wages to all faithful servants; and I am happy to say that they, as well as those at our printing establishments, with very few exceptions, have conducted themselves with great propriety.

In 1818 we purchased Springside, and in 1827 we purchased the Park estate, and erected a monument to commemorate my father's first visit to this valley, and on the very spot where he and I stood admiring the scenery below. There is a very fine view from the top of the tower on a clear day, and the Welsh hills can be descried in the distance.[1]

We attribute much of our prosperity, under Divine Providence, to the good example and good counsel of our worthy parents. They expressed a wish that I would build a Sunday School, and erect a Church to worship God in, according to the ritual of the Church of Scotland, as a tribute of gratitude to Him for His great kindness to the family. I cheerfully complied with their request, and both have been finished years ago. We have done business on a large scale, at all the places you have named, exporting our goods and receiving the productions of those countries in return; but trade for some years has been very unproductive—profits being so small, and risks so great, that we have been very much inclined to retire on the moderate fortune we have acquired with great industry, were it not to give employment to our workpeople, but we feel unwilling to throw our servants out of employment when many are only being worked three days a week.

The failure of the Grants to get work in Manchester is an indication of one of the several different characteristics which accompanied the factory system there when compared with small towns and country districts—the difference in the way labour was recruited for the new industry. Manchester was, of course, already the centre of the cotton industry and had a large population engaged in the spinning, weaving, and finishing of fustians, checks, and smallwares, and the prospect of better and more regular employment was sufficient inducement to secure an ample supply of labour for the factories.[2] Hence, the problem which confronted the country employer of how to obtain labour for his mill (the solution of which he partly found in workhouse children) never existed for the Manchester spinner.

From the first introduction of the factory system, men employed in responsible positions, such as mule spinners and mechanics, earned high wages. Men employed in the preparation rooms on work which did not demand much skill earned more than a common labourer's wage; and the employment open to women and children was better paid than in the hand processes in which so many of them had been engaged. The result was a flow of labour from other occupations into the factories.[3]

As the industry expanded, the great demand for labour was met by newcomers to the

---

[1] Grant's Tower, once a conspicuous landmark in East Lancashire, was built in 1828. It collapsed in 1944 owing to lack of repairs (*The Bury Times*, September 23, 1944).

[2] G. A. Lee listed fifty-two Manchester factories which worked with free labour before 1802 (*1816 Comm.*, p. 341).

[3] *Factories Inquiry. R. Com. Supp. Rep.* Part 1, Section D1, p. 169; 1834 (167), xix. In reply to a question as to where the first machine spinners were obtained Thomas Yates of Bolton stated:

A good many from the agricultural parts; a good many from Wales; many from Ireland and from Scotland. People left other occupations and came to spinning for the sake of the high wages. I recollect shoemakers leaving their employ and learning to spin; I recollect tailors; I recollect colliers; but a great many more husbandmen left their employ to learn to spin.

c

town, by people from the surrounding country districts, from Wales, Scotland and Ireland, who were attracted by the prospects offered by the new industry—a fact which had great influence on the social development of the town.

Before this influx had assumed great proportions, the most important social effect of the factory system was the increase it made possible in the earning power of the family. This increase was greatest in those families which had an adult male employed in a factory but, even where this was not the case, the higher earnings of women and children, who formed the majority of the personnel of the factories, meant a substantial increase in the incomes of the families to which they belonged.

When we consider the wider social aspect of the situation the question naturally arises as to whether this increased income did represent a real advance in the position of the families. Was it more than offset by the disadvantages of factory life and the home conditions in the congested working-class districts? Unfortunately an adequate answer to this question necessitates a more intimate knowledge of previous conditions than it is possible to obtain after the lapse of so long a time and in the main we have to be content with the only measure that remains, the command over the necessaries and comforts of life of families with several members in a factory. However, as the districts inhabited by operatives grew rapidly, we can surmise that in the opinion of the operatives the sordid surroundings and the evils associated with overcrowding did not offset the advantages of higher earnings.

The Wage Books of McConnel and Kennedy

Some light is thrown on these early days of the factory system by two books which are part of the material preserved by the great cotton-spinning concern of McConnel and Kennedy. The books contain the addresses of a considerable number of pickers and reelers and show that among these two sections of workpeople there was frequently more than one member of a family working for the firm. The accounts also contain the wages earned by pickers and stretchers, and when these are supplemented by wages recorded in other books belonging to the firm, and compared with such wages as are known to have been general in Manchester in 1795, they substantiate the view that the families of mill operatives at this time were in a better economic position than that of the average working-class family.[1]

An examination of the pickers' wages book suggests that few of the women listed depended entirely on their own earnings. Judging from the large number employed by the firm and the casual nature of the work of many of them, it seems probable that they worked only to augment the earnings of other members of their families. The number of hands in the employ of McConnel and Kennedy in 1795 is not known, but in 1802, when their business had grown considerably and they had made two additions to their works, they had only 312 operatives in the factory.[2] At the earlier date the number of their employees must have been much less, whereas in the eleven months covered by the book the names of over two hundred pickers are entered. A small proportion of the women worked steadily throughout the period; many had one trial and then disappeared from the book—probably those who tried

[1] Between the time when the factory system was introduced into Manchester and 1795 it is probable that the weaving of muslins and cambrics was introduced into the towns. Weavers of these cloths were in receipt of wages which would put their families in a position quite equal to those of factory workers.

[2] In 1819 McConnel and Kennedy employed 1,150 workpeople (G. W. Daniels, 'The Early Records of a Great Manchester Cotton-Spinning Firm', *Economic Journal*, June, 1915, p. 178).

the work and gave it up because of its disagreeable nature. Indeed, some of them repented their application for work very quickly for 'returned unpicked' is entered against several names. The majority of women, however, seem to have worked at intervals, probably when they could spare the time or were in urgent need of the money that could be earned.

This intermittent work was possible because picking was a hand process.[1] Premises were provided near to the mill but the pickers were not subjected to mill discipline; it appears to have been the custom to allow them to come and go as they pleased, or to take their work home if they chose to do so. This degree of liberty attracted to the employment women whose domestic duties prevented their leaving their homes for twelve hours each day, or whose health could not stand the strain of long hours of standing.[2]

As the wage book gives only the earnings of these women and of several stretchers (the reelers' book contains addresses and the quantity of work performed each day) it is impossible to obtain any definite information as to the income any particular family received from the mill. However, a knowledge of the wages paid by McConnel and Kennedy enables us to conjecture the likely income of a family which had several members employed in their works.

A family which included a spinner would be, of course, in a superior position to one whose wage earners were engaged in the preparatory processes. At this time only adult males were employed as mule spinners although some years later women were spinning on small wheels and earning about half the wage of a male spinner, an innovation which John Doherty, the leader of the operative spinners, alleged, was introduced into Manchester by McConnel and Kennedy.[3] In 1795, however, men were in undisputed possession of the occupation. Unfortunately no wage statistics of mule spinners are available for the eighteenth century. The earliest are those given for 1804 by Thomas Houldsworth[4] of Manchester, but Thomas Yates of Bolton, a witness before the Factory Commissioners, 1834, speaking of the earnings of mule spinners between 1792 and 1798, stated that they were slightly lower than those of spinners on power-driven mules in 1833.[5] In 1833 Thomas Houldsworth's fine spinners earned from 33s. 8d. to 42s. 9d. a week on counts of 180 and 200 respectively[6] which suggests that between 1792 and 1798 their earnings would be somewhere between 30s. and 38s.

Families whose earnings included those of a fine spinner were in a fortunate position but they formed only a small minority of the families dependent on the factory for their livelihood, because spinners were but a small proportion of the total employees.

[1] A minute description of the hand process is given by James Butterworth (*Complete History of the Trade of Manchester*, Manchester, 1822, pp. 95–6). Picking was performed 'by beating the cotton with sticks on a square frame, across which are stretched small cords, somewhat thicker than a goose quill, with intervals sufficient to suffer the seed, leaves, and other adventitious matter to fall through. When a hard matted, or compressed mass of cotton is smartly struck with a stick, the natural elasticity and resiliency of its fibres are gradually loosened and disengaged, and the cotton recovers by repeated strokes all its original volume. During this operation the seeds &c. which still adhere, are carefully picked out by the hand, and the cotton rendered as clean as possible'.

[2] Master Cotton Spinners, referring to these workpeople in their evidence before the 1816 Committee, stated that they were often women with children or women whose health was poor, apart from any complaint they might contract during their work. See evidence of H. Houldsworth of Glasgow (p. 238), W. Taylor, manager of 'a considerable part' of Horrocks of Preston (p. 264) and W. Sandford of Manchester (p. 367).

[3] *The Voice of the People*.

[4] See above, p. 5.

[5] *Factories Inquiry. R. Com. Supp. Rep.* Part 1, Section D1, p. 168; 1834 (167), xix.

[6] *Select Committee on Manufactures, Commerce, and Shipping*, 1833, p. 319.

McConnel and Kennedy's books afford the most valuable information about the processes preparatory to spinning in which earnings ranged from 2s. 6d. to 24s. a week. Those of women pickers who worked regularly ranged from 4s. to 8s. Weekly wages in the card room were from 3s. to the 22s. of the head carder.[1] Stretchers were paid by the piece; the earnings of men whose accounts were entered in the wage book, averaged over a period of six months from 17s. 6d. to 24s. The earnings of women stretchers varied considerably, both from week to week and as between one woman and another. One woman, whose husband or brother was also a stretcher, earned 37s. 6d. in one week and as little as 3s. 3d. in another. The earnings of a woman who worked regularly over a period of six months averaged 17s. 6d. a week, while another woman earned 21s. every week she worked. Boys and girls of ten or twelve years of age were employed as winders at 4s. 6d. a week.[2] At this time it was usual to employ younger children as scavengers in the spinning room and it is probable that McConnel and Kennedy were not exceptional in this respect, and had among their employees a number of children to whom they paid 2s. 6d. or 3s. a week.

How did these wages compare with those commonly earned in Manchester? Sir Frederick Eden in his *State of the Poor*, referring to Manchester in 1795, gives the following wages as being general in that year: 'common labourers' earned 2s. to 2s. 6d. a day; manufacturing labourers' (presumably weavers') earnings averaged about 16s. a week. Women and children employed in winding, reeling, mending and cutting fustians could earn, women up to 6s. to 12s. ('clear earnings may be stated at 8s.') a week, children of seven and eight years 2s. a week, and nine or ten years 4s. a week.[3]

A comparison of these wages with those of the employees of McConnel and Kennedy shows that the firm's workpeople were earning comparatively high wages and that the income of their families must have been considerably above that of those whose workers were in the occupations Eden mentions. It is, of course, impossible to state definitely that because one member of a family was employed in a factory the other members would also be employed there, but if one member of a family entered an occupation where the rate of remuneration was higher than that earned by the others, it seems reasonable to assume that before long they too would seek employment in the better-paid occupation. Indeed, as already mentioned, there is some evidence in McConnel and Kennedy's books to support this assumption.[4]

Eden gives the weekly earnings and expenditure of a labourer's family from which we can judge the standard of life of the unskilled workpeople who had no women or children working in a factory. The family he selected consisted of a carter aged thirty-nine, his wife aged thirty-five, and six children: three girls aged fifteen, twelve and nine years, and three boys aged five, three years and five months (Table III). The deficiency between income and expenditure was made up by the man doing odd jobs.[5]

---

[1] McConnel & Co. Ltd., *A Century of Fine Cotton Spinning*, second edition, Manchester, 1913, p. 49 The firm's weekly wage bill at the beginning of 1795 came to less than £13; before the end of 1796 it had reached £70–80.

[2] *Ibid.*, p. 38.

[3] F. M. Eden, *The State of the Poor*, Vol. II, London, 1797, p. 357.

[4] See above, p. 16.

[5] F. M. Eden, *op. cit.*, Vol. II, pp. 358–9. The eldest girl was in service and did not live at home. 'The three younger children cannot earn anything.'

TABLE III

WEEKLY BUDGET OF LABOURER'S FAMILY

Income	s.	d.	Expenditure	s.	d.
Man, carter	12	0	Rent	2	0
Wife, roving cotton about	0	6	Fuel	0	7
Girl 12, nursing for neighbour . . .	2	6	Oatmeal bread	5	0
Girl 9, nursing for neighbour	2	0	Meat	1	6
			Tea and sugar	1	3
			Potatoes	1	6
			Milk	1	2
			Butter	1	0
			Soap, candles, groceries	1	0
			Clothes and other expenses	2	0
			Cheese	1	6
	17	0		18	6

The quantities of the goods purchased are not stated but in 1795, a year of scarcity, the prices of provisions in general demand were as in Table IV.[1]

TABLE IV

PRICES OF PROVISIONS IN 1795

Loaf . .	4 lb.	. (January) 8¾d.; 1s. 1½d.	Bacon . .	1 lb.	. . . .	8d.
Wheat flour	12 lb.	. . . . . . 3s. 3d.	Potatoes .	253 lb.	. . . . . .	6s. 6d.
Oatmeal .	10 lb.	. . . . . . 1s. 11d.	Skimmed milk quart		. . . . . .	1½d.
Fresh butter	1 lb.	. . . . . . 1s. 0d.	New milk .	quart	. . . . . .	3d.
Salt butter .	1 lb.	. . . . 8d. to 10d.	Coal . .	cwt.	. . . . . 6d. to 7d.	
Beef . .	1 lb.	. . . . . 3½d. to 5d.	Candles .	1 lb.	. . . . . .	8d.
Mutton .	1 lb.	. . . . . . 5d.	Treacle . .	1 lb.	. . . (November) 5½d.	
Veal . .	1 lb.	. . . . . 5d. to 6d.	Soap . .	1 lb.	. . . (November) 10d.	
Pork . .	1 lb.	. . . . . . 5d.	Rent of two small rooms for a year .		£4 to £6	

It is evident that the amount of food bought for 18s. 6d. cannot have provided either a generous or an interesting diet for seven people. The staple articles were bread, potatoes and milk (probably skimmed), the monotony being relieved by a little butter, cheese, meat and tea. Yet if it was possible to maintain a family of six (not counting the baby of five months) on such an income, then the families which had several workers in the mill had the means to have better houses and to be better fed and clothed than this family which Eden gives as typical.

To realize this we need only consider the minimum income of a family, of which the man and two children worked regularly, employed by McConnel and Kennedy. As far as can be ascertained the lowest wage paid to men in 1795 was 16s. a week; children aged twelve and nine earned 4s. 6d. and 3s. respectively. This would make a total income of 23s. 6d. a week,

[1] The prices of the 4 lb. loaf are from *A Return of the Price of the Quartern Loaf of Wheaten Bread*, [1814–1815 (109), x], those of candles, treacle and soap from William Rowbottom, 'Chronology or Annals of Oldham' (MSS. in Oldham Public Library; transcript by Giles Shaw in the Manchester Central Library), and all others from F. M. Eden, *op. cit.*, Vol. II, p. 357. Prices are for December, 1795, except where otherwise stated.

a sum which would not have been enough to keep a family of six in comfort with prices as high as they were in 1795. But it does represent a substantial increase on 18s. 6d. The majority of men employed (the mechanics, overlookers, spinners, and stretchers) earned more than 16s. and it would appear that their families lived in more comfortable circumstances than this suppositious family.

However, in view of the great preponderance of women and children employed in cotton spinning it is important that the income of families who had an adult male in the factory should not be overstressed. The greatest number of families were in a better economic position after the introduction of the factory system because of the increased earnings of women and children.[1]

MANCHESTER AT THE TURN OF THE CENTURY

When we turn from the economic effects of the introduction of the factory system and try to picture the conditions under which the Manchester mill operatives lived, we find that, along with the rest of the working-class population of the town, they were in a very unfavourable position.

The first public protest against these conditions was made in 1792 by Dr. John Ferriar from whose report[2] it is clear that the resources of the town had been utterly inadequate to cope with the great increase in the population in the previous twenty years.[3] Housing facilities had not increased proportionately to the growth of numbers, and sanitary arrangements which had been bad when the population numbered slightly more than 22,000 were infinitely worse by 1788 when it had almost doubled.

A passage written in 1805 in which Dr. Ferriar describes the cellar dwellings in which people were crowded together owing to the lack of working-class accommodation is worth quoting:

> The number of damp, and very ill ventilated cellars inhabited in many parts of the town, is a most extensive and permanent evil . . . they consist of two rooms under ground, the front apartment of which is used as a kitchen, and though frequently noxious by its dampness, and closeness, is generally preferable to the back room: the latter has only one small window, which, though

---

[1] This point has been made by John Jones, an operative spinner of McConnel and Kennedy, in *The Cotton Mill* (Manchester, 1821):

> Now see the Cotton from the town convey'd
> To Manchester, that glorious mart of trade:
> Hail splendid scene! the Nurse of every art,
> That glads the widow's and the orphan's heart!
> Thy Mills, like gorgeous palaces, arise,
> And lift their useful turrets to the skies!
> See Kennedy's stupendous structure join'd
> To thine M'Connell—friends of human kind!
> Whose ready doors for ever wide expand
> To give employment to a numerous band,
> Murray's behold! that well deserves a name,—
> And Lee's and Houldsworth's our attention claim,—
> And numerous others, scattered up and down,
> The sole supporters of this ample town.

[2] J. Ferriar, *To the Committee for the Regulation of the Police in the Towns of Manchester and Salford*, Manchester, 1792.

[3] Manchester was estimated to have 22,481 inhabitants in 1773 and 42,821 in 1788 (F. M. Eden, *op. cit.*, Vol. II, p. 356).

on a level with the outer ground, is near the roof of the cellar, it is often covered with boards or paper, and in its best state, is so much covered with mud, as to admit little either of air or light. In this cell, the beds of the whole family, sometimes consisting of seven or eight, are placed. The floor of this room is often unpaved: the beds are fixed on the damp earth. But the floor, even when paved, is always damp. In such places, where a candle is required, even at noon-day, to examine a patient, I have seen the sick without bedsteads, lying on rags; they can seldom afford straw.[1]

The working-class dwellings which were built at the time this report was made appear to have been designed without the slightest regard for the health or convenience of their inhabitants. Dr. Ferriar deplored the fact that the practice of putting in fixed windows without any casement was becoming very common. No steps were taken to prevent this economy on the part of builders, nor had the report any effect in preventing the creation of slums; consequently as the town expanded the number of unhealthy areas constantly increased.[2]

Dr. Aikin, writing in 1795, had referred to the growth of the town and the housing of the working class:

> The new streets built within these [last] few years have nearly doubled the size of the town. Most of them are wide and spacious. . . . But . . . very few of the streets are yet flagged, which makes the walking in them, to strangers, very disagreeable. . . . As Manchester may bear comparison to the metropolis itself in the rapidity with which whole new streets have been raised, and in its extension on every side towards the surrounding country; so it unfortunately vies with, or exceeds, the metropolis, in the closeness with which the poor are crowded in offensive, dark, damp, and incommodious habitations, a too fertile source of disease![3]

The operatives employed by McConnel and Kennedy lived in the heart of industrial Manchester. Some 150 addresses are given in the books which show that most of the people to whom they referred lived in the labyrinth of streets which surrounded the works in Canal Street, or in the courts and alleys of the continuation of Piccadilly towards Ardwick Green, known as Bank Top.

These streets and the houses in them were condemned in the strongest terms by Dr. J. P. Kay in 1832[4] and although by this time they were probably in a worse state than in 1795, the conditions he described can never have been tolerable. The houses were nearly all built back-to-back, the common type of working-class house at that time. The difficulty of obtaining sufficient supplies of water must have made it impossible for the people to be cleanly in their habits. The water for cooking and drinking had to be carried from wells[5] and, as only better class houses had lead cisterns for the collection of rain water for domestic purposes,[6] the inhabitants of houses, such as those in Ancoats, had to obtain water for cleaning as best they could. The houses had no garden or yard, an inconvenience which led

[1] J. Ferriar, *Proceedings of the Board of Health in Manchester*, Manchester and London, 1805, pp. 12–3.
[2] *Loc. cit.*
[3] J. Aikin, *A Description of the Country from Thirty to Forty Miles round Manchester*, London, 1795, p. 192.
[4] J. P. Kay, *The Moral and Physical Condition of the Working Classes employed in the Cotton Manufacture in Manchester*, London, 1832, pp. 13–25.
[5] J. Aston, *The Manchester Guide*, Manchester, 1804, pp. 5–6.
[6] J. Aston (*Picture of Manchester*, Manchester, 1816, p. 4), writes: 'lately, a public company . . . have purchased the water [Shudehill pits] from the Lord of the Manor, and formed a reservoir, about two miles from the town, into which water is conveyed by the help of stone-pipes, which so frequently burst, that they are often a great nuisance, and abridge the profits on which the proprietors had calculated'.

to the insertion of a clause in the Manchester Act of 1792 forbidding the stretching of clothes lines across the streets. The streets into which the doors of the houses opened were unpaved and, as there was no provision for the systematic disposal of household rubbish, they were disfigured by heaps of refuse and pools of stagnant water. These conditions were responsible for the fever from which the town was seldom free.[1] But of the social conditions in Manchester in the 1830s something more will be said in the last chapter.

FLUCTUATIONS IN TRADE, 1810–1819

The next set of figures available relate to the period 1810–1819 and while they are of a more general character than those of the mid-1790s they do enable us, with the exercise of a little imagination, to get a broad view of the economic position of the families of cotton workers from the boom of 1810 to the end of the post-war depression.

A table, set out in the *Manchester Mercury* of January 18, 1820, evidently drawn up at the request of the Government after the disturbances of 1818–1819, gives the wages of certain sections of factory workers, handloom weavers and various kinds of labourers and craftsmen, together with the prices of provisions in each year.[2]

The general situation during these nine years has been sketched in the first chapter, but a few more details of events in Manchester will help us to interpret the table more clearly,[3] since, as the figures stand, they can hardly be said to give a fair view of the condition of the working classes during a period of great distress.

The year 1810 was one of exceptionally good trade until its close when the boom collapsed and the cotton industry was plunged into a period of depression which lasted until the later months of 1813. The situation created by the collapse of 1810 was so serious that immediately it began McConnel and Kennedy reduced the wages of all their employees.[4] It is impossible to say whether the reduction was general throughout the town but this is immaterial as the wage reductions did not keep the factories running full-time. By January, 1811, mills were working three days a week and in the next three years there were many months of short-time.[5]

1811 was the worst year for the factory workers. Nearly all of them earned only half their usual wages[6] and probably those in the employ of very small concerns were thrown out of work altogether. The plight to which this year of underemployment reduced the families of operatives is mentioned in a clause which was inserted in the Manchester weavers' petition

---

[1] In 1796 it was generally recognized that the health of all classes in Manchester was in jeopardy and, after some agitation, the Board of Health, a body supported by private subscriptions, was established (J. Aston, *Picture of Manchester*, p. 134).

[2] The table and a similar one for Glasgow are set out as Appendices II and III in G. W. Daniels, 'The Cotton Trade at the Close of the Napoleonic War', *Trans. Manch. Stat. Soc.*, 1917–1918.

[3] The story of the cotton workers during those years is told in J. L. and B. Hammond, *The Skilled Labourer, 1760–1832*, London, 1919, pp. 82–121.

[4] G. W. Daniels, 'The Cotton Trade during the Revolutionary and Napoleonic Wars', *Trans. Manch. Stat. Soc.*, 1915–1916, p. 80.

[5] McConnel and Kennedy worked the following number of days each week:

	January to June	July to December
1811	3	$3\frac{1}{2}$
1812	5	6 (full-time)
1813	4	6 (full-time)

(McConnel & Co. Ltd., *A Century of Fine Cotton Spinning*, p. 52).

[6] There was at least one exception. Philips and Lee ran full-time throughout the period (*1816 Comm.*, p. 340).

of 1811. The House of Commons was entreated 'to take into their consideration the distress and situation of the different mechanical branches in general, who are, for want of employment, reduced to want and misery, as the scanty pittance of their earnings is wholly inadequate to procure them the common necessaries of life, the majority of them not being employed more than three days per week'.[1] Although the earnings of the factory workers in the next two years were reduced by short time they were in a considerably better position than in 1811.

The weavers fared far worse. They were more numerous than the factory operatives, and the amount of work available was insufficient to find even part-time employment for the whole of them. The severe losses on cloth owing to the fall in prices ruined many of their employers and compelled those that continued manufacturing to put out work at much lower prices. The Bolton petition recited 'not more than two-thirds of the looms of the petitioners are employed . . . [and], that, on a fair average, they cannot earn more than 5s. per week'.[2] In their appeal to Parliament for help the Manchester weavers stated that 'the great bulk of the Petitioners are reduced to the most dreadful situation, beyond all former precedent and example, great numbers experiencing the total want of employ, and thousands daily suffering the absolute want of the necessaries of life, for themselves, their wives, and helpless offspring'.[3]

Even when due allowance is made for the fact that petitions are hardly unbiased statements of fact, there can be no doubt that the majority of the families solely dependent on weaving were in a state of abject poverty during 1811 and 1812. In the former year their distress was aggravated by high prices. Food riots occurred in the town. These were suppressed by the military and the weavers then sought to avenge their sufferings by the destruction of power looms. They succeeded in burning a factory at Middleton at the cost of ten lives.[4]

Trade appears to have improved in the later months of 1813 and on the conclusion of the war was very brisk for a short time, the activity being reflected in the weavers' wages. The following year their wages fell once more and did not recover in the period covered by the table. In 1816 there was a general turnout of spinners, colliers and weavers for an advance in wages and on September 9 Gray's factory was attacked and a man killed.[5] In 1818 all the spinners in Manchester turned out for the old rates alleging that their wages had been 'very inadequate to procure even the coarsest necessaries of Life' and that they had 'been obliged by degrees to part with our Goods and Clothing' to buy food.[6] It is stated that by June 18, 20,000 Manchester factory hands were on strike. The actual number of spinners seems to have been in the region of 2,200.[7]

[1] *Hansard*, May 30, 1811, p. 341.

[2] *Ibid.*, p. 342. On June 13 a Commons' Committee, having 'carefully and maturely examined' the petition reported that, while fully acknowledging 'the great distress of numbers of persons engaged in the cotton manufacture', it was 'decidedly of opinion, that grants of pecuniary aid, to any particular class of persons suffering under temporary distress, would be utterly inefficacious as to every good purpose, and most objectionable in all points of view; particularly as they could not fail of exciting expectations unbounded in extent, incapable of being realized, and most likely to destroy the equilibrium of labour and of employment, in the various branches of manufacture, of commerce, and agriculture'.

[3] *Hansard*, May 30, 1811, p. 341.

[4] G. W. Daniels, 'The Cotton Trade at the Close of the Napoleonic War', *Trans. Manch. Stat. Soc.*, 1917–1918, p. 10.

[5] W. E. A. Axon, *The Annals of Manchester*, Manchester and London, 1886, p. 155.

[6] J. L. and B. Hammond, *op. cit.*, p. 97, citing H.O., 42.178.

[7] *Loc. cit.*

EARNINGS AND COST OF LIVING IN MANCHESTER, 1810–1819

No mention of the fluctuations in trade is made in the table printed in the *Manchester Mercury*[1] which ostensibly was published as a general statement of the earnings of Manchester cotton workers during the years 1810–1819. The actual earnings of fine spinners are given as well as the average earnings of coarse spinners, but no change is recorded in either between 1814 and 1819. If this were the case it would mean that the reduction of 1816 was made up by increased production and did not diminish the income of the spinners—a view which the spinners' strike in 1818 would hardly substantiate. However, the conflicting statements of employers and men do not carry us much further, so we have to accept the figures set out in the table with the reservation that after 1816 it probably overstates the earnings of the majority of the spinners.

In the case of the weavers the table is still more misleading since their earnings are given as though they were fully employed. The result is a sum which they might have earned had there been work for them to do, not their actual earnings. In the years when work was scarce the earnings of those who succeeded in obtaining some employment cannot have approached the amount given as the average weekly earnings of weavers.

It will be seen, therefore, that the wage statistics are rather on the high side and that any conclusions based upon them, especially in the case of the weavers, must also err in the same direction. However, as they are the only figures of a general character that relate to these years they have been supplemented by other details of wages and prices which appear to be more realistic and an attempt has been made in Appendix B Tables III–VII to show the condition of the families of cotton workers during these years.

Bread has been excluded from Table VI because its high price must have taken it almost out of reach of the poorer working-class families. When bread forms the basis of the diet 40 lb. a week is a moderate allowance for a family of six. During these years the 4 lb. loaf was nearly always over 1s. and sometimes as much as 1s. 6d. and 1s. 8d.; consequently the diet for a family of this size would have meant an expenditure of from 10s. to 15s. (or more) a week for bread alone. Probably all families bought some bread but for our purpose it seems best to calculate the cost of the very cheapest food and for this reason bread has been eliminated altogether and oatmeal made the basis of the diet.

Even if we leave clothes and household goods out of our reckoning, as commodities the purchase of which can be entirely suspended in bad times, we must add rent, coal, candles, soap and a small allowance for miscellaneous expenses to the cost of food if we are to make up a weekly household budget. These items would take another 5s. 9d. a week, allowing 2s. 9d. for rent, 1s. 6d. for coal and candles, and 1s. 6d. for soap and sundries.[2] In Table VII the total cost of maintaining this very modest standard of life is given for each year, together with the income of five suppositious families.

[1] January 18, 1820.

[2] The weekly rents paid by the working classes in Manchester at the time of an enquiry carried out during 1834–1836 were as follows:

Rent		No. of		Rent		No. of
s. d.	s. d.	Houses		s. d.	s. d.	Houses
Under	1 0	184		3 0½ to	3 6	3,121
1 0½ to	1 6	2,935		3 6½ to	4 0	1,614
1 6½ to	2 0	3,585		4 0½ and over		6,895
2 0½ to	2 6	4,913				———
2 6½ to	3 0	4,939			Total	28,186

This table cannot do more than attempt to show the probable income of certain families, and to indicate the amount that could be bought with their income in different years. It will be seen that in 1811 only families who worked in the best paid jobs in factories could have lived at the standard implied by the budget and that the statement in the Manchester petitions that the factory workers were unable to obtain sufficient food for their families with the 'scanty pittance' they were earning, was no exaggeration of the condition of the vast majority of them in that year.[1] During the years covered by the table, 1810–1819, the families of spinners were not in this wretched state again; indeed, throughout the period, with the exception of the early months of 1813, they were able to live in much greater comfort than this budget would allow, while families with a woman and two young children in a factory could have lived, with the exception of the three bad years 1811–1813, at a slightly higher standard than the one assumed in the budget.

On the other hand the income of the weaving family never enabled it to live up to this standard and only in the boom years 1810 and 1814 could a weaving family with two young children in a mill live as well as this. The budget could, of course, be cut considerably before the families were in a hopeless position and this point would not be reached by the families pictured above. But in the years when a fully employed weaver was an exception incomes calculated on the basis of full employment do not afford much insight into what actually obtained.

A better perception of what was endured by a large proportion of the families of cotton workers during 1811–1812 and from the latter months of 1815 to the end of the period can be got from the columns of the newspapers, where the charitable efforts of the middle classes are noted, and from the reports of the Overseers about the amount paid in relief.[2] The melancholy story is completed in the annual *Report of the Board of Health in Manchester*:[3]

It is well known, that, during the years 1817 and 1818, *contagious fevers* raged, with remarkable violence, in almost every part of England, Ireland and Scotland;—and it could hardly be expected that the large and crowded towns of Manchester and Salford, containing so great a proportion of the poorer classes of society, would entirely escape from the influence of so widely spreading an epidemic. For, if we consider the probable causes of the unusual prevalence of those diseases at the periods just mentioned;—the remarkably wet seasons, the deficient harvests, and the injured state of the grain in 1816 and 1817,—with the dreadful distresses of the times, by which

---

[1] *Hansard*, May 30, 1811, p. 341.
[2] The amount of poor relief paid in Manchester was as follows:

	£		£
1810–1811	24,853	1815–1816	23,848
1811–1812	33,000	1816–1817	53,748
1812–1813	45,511	1817–1818	43,640
1813–1814	33,129	1818–1819	31,567
1814–1815	20,919		

(G. W. Daniels, 'The Cotton Trade at the Close of the Napoleonic War' (Appendix II), *Trans. Manch. Stat. Soc.*, 1917–1918).
[3] Manchester, 1819, p. 3.

These 28,186 dwellings—21,453 houses, 3,162 single rooms and 3,571 cellars—housed 128,232 persons, 15,474 of whom were employed in cotton factories. 14,144 dwellings having a table, chairs, a clock, a chest of drawers and a fair stock of utensils were classified as 'well furnished'. 14,042 dwellings did not achieve this minimum. The enquiry covered 64 per cent of the population of Manchester (*Report of A Committee of the Manchester Statistical Society on the Condition of the Working Classes in an extensive manufacturing district, in 1834, 1835 and 1836*, London, 1838, Read at the Statistical Section of the British Association for the Advancement of Science, Liverpool, 1837).

many of the labouring poor were deprived of a sufficiency, not only of food, but of clothing, firing, and shelter;—we shall rather feel disposed to wonder that our two populous towns had not a still greater share of the general calamity;—as the exciting causes undoubtedly existed here in a degree hardly less than in any other part of England.

It is evident that we have here a part—possibly a large part—of the explanation of the rapidity with which political reformers gained recruits in the manufacturing centres. The short shrift meted out to Lancashire men suspected of holding advanced political views showed that the Government quite appreciated the nature of the highly inflammable material which poverty and despair were piling up. It never blazed—not because of the measures taken by the Government—but because reviving trade and a good harvest retrieved the situation.

CHAPTER IV

A COUNTRY FACTORY
BURRS MILL, BURY, 1801–1802

BURY AND THE PEEL FAMILY

ACCORDING to the census of 1801 Bury, then a small country town nine miles north of Manchester, contained 1,341 inhabited houses occupied by 1,400 families, and the total population numbered 7,072 persons of whom 107 were engaged in agriculture, 4,545 in manufactures and handicrafts, and 2,420 not classified.

At the time this census was taken Bury was the seat of the Peels, one of the pioneer firms in the textile industry and one which had attracted many newcomers to the town. Before the remarkable development of the cotton industry and the finishing trade Bury could claim the title of 'town' only by courtesy, having in 1773 but 463 houses and 2,090 inhabitants.[1] In 1801 practically the whole of the wage-earning population was engaged in the manufacture and finishing of textile goods, principally cotton. At the earlier date the cotton manufacture was in its infancy and the woollen industry, the long established staple trade of the town, though challenged, was still the most important industry.

The fact that the woollen industry was widespread is borne out by the number of men who still carried on the manufacture in 1816 when the cotton and printing industries had already made the fortunes of several families. It is recorded in a Bury directory for that year that the town then had thirty-five woollen manufacturers, fourteen cotton manufacturers, six calico printers and four bleachers.[2] The woollen industry, however, was rapidly eclipsed by the cotton industry when Robert Peel and his partner, William Yates, were able, with the aid of Arkwright machinery to spin, manufacture and print large quantities of cotton goods.

Bury was one of the earliest towns to experience the changes which accompanied the organization of industry on a large scale. The establishment of the concern, of which Robert Peel, 1750–1830 (the first baronet), became the head, marked a new era in the industrial and social development of the town.[3]

The exact date at which the printing trade began at Bury is somewhat obscure and, unfortunately, many details of the early history of the Peels and their partners are matters of conjecture.

There are, for example, several versions of the way in which the first Robert Peel, a farmer and a woollen weaver, became a printer. One of them, given by Sir Lawrence Peel,

---

[1] J. Aikin, *op. cit.*, p. 266.

[2] F. Howarth, ' "I Remember." Some Notes on Old Bury', reprinted from *Bury Guardian*, 1917, pp. 50–1.

[3] An interesting account of what this change meant is given in a series of papers, *Walks Round Bury for Sixty Years and Upwards*, Bury, 1842, by a Bury hatter, John Ainsworth, who wrote under the pseudonym of 'Veritas'. He bitterly regretted the changes wrought by the growth of industry, and looked back with longing to the days when country gentlemen made modest fortunes in the woollen or fustian trade, and lived contentedly in the town, taking that interest in local affairs which becomes a man and a gentleman.

asserts that William Haworth, a brother-in-law of Peel, was apprenticed to a London calico printer and, knowing that the heavy cotton goods made in the Blackburn district were sent to London to be finished, determined, on his return to Blackburn at the close of his apprenticeship, to start printing in Lancashire. He was joined in his venture by the first Robert Peel who raised some capital by mortgaging his farm. The amount, however, was insufficient and they found another partner in William Yates, the son of a Blackburn publican, who is said to have brought £500 into the business.[1]

According to another story, the profits to be derived from calico printing were demonstrated to Peel through his having a piece of cloth which had been spoilt in weaving printed by the firm of Clayton of Bamber Bridge, and then selling it cut up into handkerchiefs.[2]

Whichever story is true—if either is—it is a fact that Robert Peel of Blackburn started printing in partnership with William Haworth and William Yates, though the partnership cannot have lasted very long as Haworth soon left to start in business at Bury. Here he was joined by a man named Yates, whether the one mentioned above or another is not known.[3] Apparently they must have come to Bury in the late '60s as the Claytons of Bamber Bridge, the first calico printers in Lancashire, established their works in 1764 and Peel started printing at Blackburn after that date. Peel's son, Robert, left him to join the Bury firm about 1773.[4] Twenty years later he had amassed a fortune in industry sufficiently large to enable him, in 1797, to present the Government with £10,000 to help replenish the Exchequer suffering under the strain of four years of war, and in 1800 he became a baronet.[5]

In 1773, the year in which he had become a partner, the firm began spinning and manufacturing the calico upon which, when printed, it built up its reputation. The first factory established was a small one, equipped with hand jennies, in Butcher's Lane, Bury.[6] Before long the firm had two spinning mills driven by water power. One mill at Radcliffe and one at Hinds employed weavers in North and East Lancashire,[7] while the print works underwent continuous expansion. In 1783 a print works was established at Ramsbottom[8] and shortly afterwards four more spinning mills were acquired.[9]

The remarkable progress of the concerns run by Robert Peel and his partners, the huge fortunes made by the original proprietors which enabled several of them to enter the ranks of the landed gentry and Peel to found a county family and take an active interest in politics, are well-known facts, but little is known of the factory community they created on the banks of the Irwell.

In a wage book belonging to the firm we are able to obtain an idea of some aspects of the life lived by the factory hands at Bury, as it gives a fairly complete account of the earnings and expenditure of a number of the employees.[10] The information relates to 136 persons

[1] Sir Lawrence Peel, *Life and Character of Sir Robert Peel*, London, 1860, pp. 16–7; Samuel Smiles, *Self-Help*, London, 1876, p. 39. See also 'The Peel Family', a series of articles in the *Supplement* to *The Manchester Examiner and Times*, October 5 to November 16, 1850.

[2] 'The Peel Family', *Supplement* to *The Manchester Examiner and Times*, October 12, 1850.

[3] F. Espinasse, *Lancashire Worthies*, Second Series, London, 1877, p. 84.

[4] J. Ainsworth, *op. cit.*, p. 64.

[5] *Gentleman's Magazine*, 1830, p. 556; *D.N.B.*

[6] J. Ainsworth, *op. cit.*, p. 71.

[7] 'The Peel Family', *Supplement* to *The Manchester Examiner and Times*, October 12, 1850.

[8] W. Hume Elliot, *op. cit.*, p. 117.

[9] The mills are described by J. Aikin, *op. cit.*, pp. 268–9.

[10] The Burrs Mill wage book (No. 31989) is in Chetham's Library, Manchester.

employed at Burrs Mill (one of the firm's spinning mills near Bury), and for the two years it covers, 1801–1802, it gives sufficient details to enable us to compare their earnings with other wage statistics and to know something of the standard of life of the families to which they belonged. Moreover, it is probable that Burrs Mill can safely be considered as typical of the six spinning mills in which the firm produced yarn for their calico.[1]

THE BURRS MILL WAGE BOOK

The Burrs Mill wage book covers the period November, 1800, to January, 1803, and, if the wage-earning labour constituted the whole of the employees, it would appear that the mill was a very small one. However, it seems likely that the wage labour was only a small proportion of the total number of employees. The remainder would probably consist of pauper apprentices who received food, clothing and lodging in return for their labour. In the wage book there is no direct evidence that these children were employed at the mill, the only references to apprentices being two entries of small sums paid to a woman 'for apprentices', but there is definite evidence which establishes the fact in a story told by 'Veritas' in *Walks Round Bury*.[2]

There does not seem to be any possibility of estimating the number of apprentices but, from the importance Sir Robert Peel attached to their labour, it is clear that the cotton industry in Bury was largely dependent on them at this time, and that free labour formed only a small proportion of the workers employed in his mills. He repeatedly emphasized this point when giving evidence before the *Select Committee on the State of the Children employed in the Manufactories* in 1816.[3] With this explanation of the very small number of operatives whose names are entered in the wage book we can pass on to examine the accounts in more detail.

In the wage book each family was allocated a double page. On the credit side the earnings of each member were entered separately, together with information about whether he or she were on day or piece work, the number of days worked, and the total earnings of the family. On the other side were debited the sums which they owed to the firm. Often these items swallowed up the entire income and sometimes the earnings were not sufficient to discharge the liabilities. As a rule, however, there was something left to be handed over in cash. An immense amount of bookkeeping was involved and perhaps owing to this reason the book was made up fortnightly.

[1] For conflicting accounts concerning conditions at the Radcliffe mill see the *Manchester Mercury*, October 19 to November 30 and December 28, 1784, and anon, 'The putrid fever at Robert Peel's Radcliffe Mill' (*Notes and Queries*, Vol. 203, January 1958, pp. 26–35).

[2] The story relates that a set of apprentices from a distant part of the country were told, on their arrival at Burrs 'prentice house, to light the kitchen fire. They obeyed this instruction but gained notoriety by mistaking oat cakes, which were drying on the mantlepiece, for firewood (p. 66).

[3] Asked whether he employed parish apprentices Peel replied, 'There were no others I could get' (p. 135). 'When Arkwright's machinery had first an existence', he went on, 'steam power was but little known, and . . . those who wished to . . . benefit by those improvements, resorted to country places where there were great waterfalls, and consequently could not have any other than apprentice labour; and I was in that situation for I had no other' (p. 141).

An indenture of December, 1802, signed by the churchwardens of St. Luke's Parish, Middlesex, shows that Yates received £4 2s. 0d.—£2 0s. 0d. to be paid in seven weeks and £2 2s. 0d. when the apprentice, Frances Parker, had served three years (W. Nicholls, *History and Traditions of Radcliffe*, Manchester and London, 1910, p. 174).

The 'debits' consisted of purchases, apparently made at a shop kept by the firm, of rent when the employees lived in one of the firm's cottages (nineteen out of the twenty-five families did so), and the cash balance, if any. The records enable us to see how a great proportion of the families whose members worked at the mill spent their income. The following extracts relate to the Brooks family:

TABLE V

A FAMILY BUDGET FROM THE BURRS MILL WAGE BOOK

May 8, 1802.	£	s.	d.		£	s.	d.
Samuel 12 days	1	8	0	Cash	0	3	11
Robert 12¾ days	0	15	11	Shop goods	1	18	2
Squire 12¾ days	0	8	6	Rent	0	2	6
Rachel 12 days	0	10	0	Cash	0	3	0
James 12¾ days	0	5	4	Cash	0	4	0
Ann, spinning	1	2	6½	Mr. Haworth	0	10	0
Peggy, spinning	0	16	1	Cash	3	4	11
Alice, cotton picking	1	0	1½				
	£6	6	6		£6	6	6

This family enjoyed a larger income than any other employed by the firm. Five of its workers were adults and it was fortunate in that two of them were spinners. Their average weekly income for 1802 was £2 8s. 1½d.

Besides items of rent, shop goods and cash, which appear every fortnight, and the amount paid towards the goods obtained on credit, which appear frequently, there are, during 1801, three payments in each account to a funeral club, as well as a similar payment in 1802. Payments were also made irregularly for meat, coals and potatoes, and, occasionally, for cloth, print and sheets. Several of the women had money deducted for 'bedgowns'. Whether the firm sold these ready made or as lengths of calico is not stated, the book-keeper simply entering 'bedgown 4s. 6d.'.

When an examination is made of the articles sold by Peel, Yates and Peel to their work-people we can see how dependent the operatives were on their employers for the satisfaction of their daily wants: for house room, food, and in many cases for fuel and clothing. As is well known, this system, under which the employer supplied as many of the wants of his hands as possible, often led to grave abuses, and in the early 1840s the manufacturers of Bury and its neighbourhood were accused of being responsible for the lack of thrift and forethought which was said to be characteristic of the factory population where this system prevailed.[1]

It seems hardly credible, however, that a firm of the dimensions of Peel, Yates and Peel in 1801–1802 would trouble itself with the minute details of retail shopkeeping, solely because of the profit that could be made. More likely, owing to the rapid growth of a large works in the neighbourhood of a small market town, the firm had to make some provision for the numerous people it encouraged to migrate to Bury.

The firm's mills were spread over a wide area, miles away from one another.[2] The

---

[1] Evidence of Dr. P. M. M'Douall before *Select Committee on Payment of Wages*, 1842, pp. 96–107.
[2] For the several mills see pp. 28.

principal concern was the print works and the bleaching ground, which were not far from the present-day centre of Bury, and here so many houses had to be erected that a small colony was formed on the outer ring of what was then the town. There is no record that the firm supplied any wants of their hands engaged at the print works apart from providing these houses. The spinning mills, however, were a considerable distance from the print works; Burrs Mill stood a mile and a half from the centre of Bury, and with the mill running night and day and a minimum working day of twelve hours, exclusive of meal times,[1] the operatives would hardly have the opportunity or, perhaps, in many cases, the desire to traverse three miles to make their purchases.

EARNINGS AT BURRS MILL

The greater part of the labour employed at Burrs Mill was paid on a time basis. The rate of pay for women and girls varied from 4d. to 1s. 6d. a day but very few women received more than 1s. 2d.; those who did were probably in a position of responsibility. The boys and men earned from 4d. to 3s. 4d. a day. The small number of adult male workers suggests that the men employed were the joiners and mechanics necessary for the running and repair of machinery. Indeed, employment in Burrs Mill must have been a blind-alley occupation for boys, and several who evidently reached their maximum wage during the years covered by the book left the mill, presumably to seek work which offered better prospects.

A glance at the earnings of day workers over a period reveals that practically all of them received increases of pay at intervals until they reached the maximum. The wage book records several contracts made between parents and the firm and the usual arrangement seems to have been for very youthful workers to receive a certain wage for twelve months, followed by increases of 6d. a week every six months. For instance, on December 1, 1801, it is recorded:

John Chadwick engages his children to work at Burrs Mill 11 months as under

Robert 5s. 0d. a week 6 months and 5 months 5s. 6d.
Susan   5s. 6d. ,,   ,, ,,   ,,   ,, ,,   ,,   6s. 0d.
Sally   4s. 0d. ,,   ,, 11   ,,
Edward 2s. 6d. ,,   ,, ,,   ,,

This rate of increase was customary but not universal, for some day workers received rises more rapidly. Thus Betty Cook earned 8d. a day in November, 1800, and received increases of 1d. a day in February, October and December, 1801, and in January and April, 1802. The explanation of this is probably to be found in the type of the work performed but the wage book does not give any indication of the processes on which day workers were engaged.

The casual nature of the work of some of the people employed in the mill is very striking and it is noticeable that in no case of these was any other member of their families employed there. It will be seen from the short periods worked by the persons whose records are given in Table VI, that their employment was very irregular and this stands in striking contrast to the steady work of the majority of the families employed at Burrs Mill.

---

[1] Peel's evidence before *1816 Comm.*, p. 137.

D

TABLE VI

CASUAL LABOUR AT BURRS MILL

WOMEN AND GIRLS

Period Worked		Weekly Wage
2 months, 1800		4s. 0d.
3 months, 1801	Mary Bamford	5s. 6d.
7 months, 1802		6s. 0d.
1 month		
1 month	Catherine Giles	7s. 0d.
3 months	Mary Hall	7s. 0d.
1 month	Rachel Bentley	6s. 6d.
2 months	Alice Pearson	4s. 0d.
4 months	Martha Hattlebarrow	6s. 9d.
9 months	Betty Lomax	10s. 0d.
2 months	Peggy Ashworth	7s. 0d.
7 months	Ann Hardman	6s. 0d.
7 months	Nancy Ray	6s. 0d.
2 months	Mary Spender	6s. 0d.

MEN AND BOYS

Period Worked		Weekly Wage
8 months	Thomas Harrison	18s. 0d.
3 months	John Booth	15s. 0d.
4 months	John Turner	16s. 0d.
8 months	Thomas Bentley	14s. 0d.
6 weeks	Robert Wood	8s. 6d.
3 months	John Greenhalgh	6s. 0d.
11 months	George Booth	6s. 0d.
3 months	William Fenton	4s. 6d.
4 months	William Warburton	6s. 0d.
2 weeks	William Meadowcroft	5s. 6d.

Cotton picking, batting, roving, and spinning were paid by the piece. There was little difference in the earning power of the women employed in picking cotton: the wages of six women, chosen at random and averaged over six months, ranged from 8s. 3d. to 8s. 8d. a week. The price paid for rovings was 1s. 2d. for 100 lb., and the weekly wage of a man working steadily averaged about 14s. 6d. The earnings of spinners varied considerably; the less expert who alternated their spinning with day work earned about 6s. 9d. a week when spinning, and 6s. 6d. or 7s. when on day work. Whole-time spinners earned, taking an average of six months, the lowest 9s. 6d. and the highest 12s. weekly.

Ninety-five of the workers belonged to twenty-six families, and the accounts were made up in a way which enables the income from the mill going to each family to be calculated without difficulty. The income of each family depended, of course, upon the number and age of its workers and the work on which they were engaged. Table VII shows the income of six of the families with the greatest earning power, each family having five workers in the mill, during the six months January to June, 1801.[1]

[1] The ages of the workpeople have been decided by comparing their earnings with those given in Dr. James Mitchell's analysis of the earnings of 3,770 cotton operatives in 1833 (*Factories Inquiry. R. Com. Supp. Rep.* Part I, pp. 21, 33; 1834 (167), xix).

TABLE VII

INCOME OF SIX FAMILIES WITH THE GREATEST EARNING POWER AT BURRS MILL, 1801

Family	Age and Sex	Occupation	Average Weekly Income
			£ s. d.
Brierley . .	Man, youth, girl, two women .	1 batter; 2 dayworkers; 2 spinners	1 15 9
Crossley . .	Three women, youth, boy . .	1 cotton picker; 2 day workers; 2 spinners	1 18 0
Brooks . . .	Three women (one works 3 months)	1 cotton picker; 2 day workers; 2 spinners (one alternates spinning and day work)	1 6 6
Pollitt . . .	Man, woman, girl, two boys. .	All on day work	1 7 10
Barlow . . .	Three women, two girls . . .	1 cotton picker; 2 day workers; 2 spinners	1 14 3
Wood . . .	Two women, youth, two boys .	1 cotton picker; 4 day workers .	1 3 11

It would be interesting to know the type of work performed for these wages but apart from batting, roving, and spinning, there is no mention of the processes in which the operatives were engaged. However, as it seems certain that the mill was equipped with Arkwright machinery, all the day workers, with the exception of the children employed as bobbin doffers, must have been occupied in the carding and slubbing rooms. Batting, or picking, was still a hand process and although the women employed as pickers at Burrs Mill worked more regularly than those of McConnel and Kennedy, an examination of the earnings of the families reveals that the occupation attracted the rather casual type of worker.

HOUSING, EXPENDITURE AND COST OF LIVING

The entries in the Burrs Mill wage book leave much to surmise. Three items entered every pay day are rent, shop goods and cash. At irregular intervals items appear relating to 'notes', or to some article which had been bought from, or through, the firm.

In every case the rent comes to 1s. 3d. a week but, on occasion, the firm appears to have allowed one or two families who were in difficulties to pay half the rent. The accommodation provided consisted of a two-roomed cottage in a row of twenty back-to-back cottages. The cottages were built by the firm to house the workers at the mill, and are still in existence (in the 1960s) though but two or three are inhabitable. Apparently they originally had no gardens attached to them[1] but this was not a serious defect in view of their situation in a valley which, despite the growth of Bury, still preserves its pleasantly wooded hills, and a river—now, unfortunately, heavily polluted.

[1] One family rented a 'garden' from the firm for 2s. 6d. a year, but this would be a small allotment some distance from the cottage.

When the cottages were inspected in 1920 for the purpose of this thesis, no trace could be found of any facilities for housework. Four walls and a fireplace seem to have sufficed for domestic arrangements of the occupants. Water must have been obtained from the river or a neighbouring spring, and no provision existed for the systematic disposal of water or refuse. Apparently earth formed the floor of the lower room in each house, though possibly it may have sometimes been bricked or flagged. The upper room was reached by a wooden staircase from the lower room, both rooms being exactly the same size. If the households consisted only of those members of the family entered in the wage book—which is improbable—the two rooms must have accommodated in many cases at least five or six people.

An item of regular appearance in all the accounts, with exception of those of employees who were paid in cash, relates to 'shop-goods'. These were goods purchased at the shop owned by the firm but, unfortunately, we know nothing of the content. It is probable, however, that they were groceries, for other articles were entered separately, and if the amounts spent at the shop in 1801 and 1802 are compared, it is clear that the goods bought must have been the absolute necessities of life. The other articles bought from the firm were print, sheets, coal, potatoes (during the dearth of 1801) and meat in each year during the months of September to December.

The amount received in cash varied considerably and there is no clue as to the way in which it was spent. The next item, 'notes', is, however, more informative. These were issued to the employees by the firm and apparently enabled them to purchase goods on credit from the shopkeeper to whom they were made out, the debt being thus guaranteed by Peel, Yates and Peel. The account was then settled by means of a small sum being stopped out of the workers' wages and paid to the tradespeople every fortnight. The articles bought in this way were household goods—pots and pans, blankets, and, possibly, furniture; also clothes and shoes—things within reach when food was plentiful and cheap, but which were cut down to a minimum in times of scarcity.

The names of sixteen shopkeepers appear in the wage book, and if it were possible to discover the type of goods they sold we might hazard a guess as to the way the notes were used. However, only three can be traced. With a bootmaker a brisk trade was carried on, notes to 'R. Crompton' being very frequent; a butcher appeared very seldom and then only for small amounts. Perhaps the most interesting entries were those under the name of 'Mr. Grant', a draper whose sons, William and David, had a remarkable industrial career and were immortalized as the Brothers Cheeryble in *Nicholas Nickleby*. Their warehouse was in Cannon Street, Manchester. Obviously the notes to the shoemaker and Grant indicate that the purchases to which they referred were of shoes and drapery, possibly clothing, but as regards the others—apart from these to the butcher—it is difficult to form an opinion. It is improbable, however, that they referred to provisions, as these were bought from the shop kept by the firm. The impression one gets is that the notes were used to purchase household goods.

A study of the amounts debited against twenty families and the amounts received in cash during the six months, January to June, 1801, shows the weekly average of the purchases at the shop as well as the rent and cash received. The sum debited (which included miscellaneous goods and the subscription to the funeral club) usually, though not always, corresponded with the amount earned. Although in the majority of cases there is no evidence to enable us to form an opinion as to whether the income earned at the mill constituted the entire income of the family,[1] one fact is clear—a large proportion of earnings was spent on groceries.

The first half of 1801 includes some of the most economically difficult months of the war for the civilian population.[2] The country, after two years of scarcity, was suffering from a food shortage which had raised prices to the highest point they touched during the war period. The severe winter of 1798–1799, followed by the failure of the harvest and heavy rain in August, 1800, ruined half of what had promised to be a plentiful harvest.[3] The price of wheat, barley and oats rose rapidly from May, 1799, and, after a slight fall in July and August, 1800, reached the maximum in March, 1801. The prices per quarter during these years of famine are given in Table VIII compiled from Tooke's *History of Prices*.[4]

Flour and oatmeal were, of course, the principal articles in the diet of the working classes but there were many other minor articles, of which prices are difficult to obtain, but which would certainly be bought by every housewife until the family consumption had to be cut down to the lowest level of subsistence. This point was certainly not reached by the workers at Burrs Mill, although their grocery bills absorbed a large proportion of their incomes. In the pamphlets written during 1800–1801, explaining or suggesting remedies for the scarcity, there are many references to the increase in the cost of all articles of general consumption but unfortunately the writers do not state in detail to what the increased prices referred or the amount of the increases. We know that butter, cheese, bacon, the coarser parts of meat,[5] sugar, tea, salt, wool, leather[6] and potatoes all increased in price during those years, either from the great demand for foodstuffs to take the place of the scarce and expensive cereals, or because of increased taxation.

In an account book kept by the Sutton Poor House[7] during 1797–1798 and the early months of 1799 there are several lists giving the prices of many of these articles before the scarcity. To judge from the size of its grocery order, the institution must have been on a very small scale, and probably would not have had any considerable advantage over the most modest householders in making its purchases; consequently the prices given may be considered a fair criterion of current prices. When compared with the prices for 1800–1802 given in William Rowbottom's 'Chronology' or 'Annals of Oldham' it is clear that, unaccompanied by any change in the rate of wages, the high prices must have involved a great deterioration in the standard of living. Table IX gives the prices of ordinary household goods before, during, and after the scarcity.

The scarcity evidently roused people to make an effort to relieve the food shortage by growing potatoes and, with supplies forthcoming in large quantities, the price fell from an average of 15s. 6d. a load in 1800 to 6s. a load in 1801. In March and May, 1801, after potatoes had been 1s. 8d. a score for ten months, Peel, Yates and Peel sold potatoes to

[1] The exceptions are cases, of which there are several, where contracts are made by fathers on behalf of their children. Presumably these fathers would also be wage earners.

[2] G. W. Daniels, 'The Cotton Trade during the Revolutionary and Napoleonic Wars', *Trans. Manch. Stat. Soc.*, 1915–1916, p. 62.

[3] Thomas Tooke, *A History of Prices*, London, 1838, Vol. I, pp. 213, 217.

[4] *Ibid.*, Vol. I, pp. 214, 216–8, 224, 237, 251.

[5] T. R. Malthus, *An Investigation of The Cause of the Present High Price of Provisions*, London, 1800, p. 12.

[6] T. Tooke, *op. cit.*, Vol. I, pp. 224–5.

[7] Sutton, Macclesfield, Cheshire. The account book (No. 31,987) is in Chetham's Library, Manchester.

TABLE VIII

PRICES OF GRAIN DURING FAMINE YEARS, 1799–1803

	1799		1800			1801			1802	1803
	May	December	June	August	December	March	June	December	December	December
	s. d.	s. d.	s. d.	s. d.	s. d.	s. d.	s. d.	s. d.	s. d.	s. d.
Wheat	61 8	94 2	134 5	96 2	133 0	156 2	129 8	75 6	57 1	52 3
Barley	35 0	45 5	69 1	54 3	76 7	90 7	69 7	44 0	25 7	23 11
Oats	27 4	33 3	51 1	35 9	41 8	47 2	37 2	23 4	20 0	21 1

TABLE IX

PRICES OF FOODSTUFFS, 1797–1802[1]

		January, 1797	January, 1798	January, 1799	May, 1800	January, 1801	January, 1802
Meal	peck	1s. 4d.	1s. 3d.	1s. 6d. to 1s. 9d.	4s. 10d. to 5s. 2d.	4s. 4d. to 4s. 10d.	2s. 0d. to 2s. 1d.
Flour	peck	1s. 8d.		1s. 1d. to 2s. 0d.	4s. 6d. to 5s. 6d.	5s. 4d. to 5s. 8d.	2s. 8d. to 2s. 10d.
Potatoes	score	6½d.	8d.	5½d.	1s. 8d.	1s. 8d.	6d.
Old butter	lb.	9d.		9d.	1s. 2d.	1s. 3d.	9d.
New butter	lb.			11d.			
Cheese	lb.	6d. to 7d.	10d.	5d. to 6d.	9d.	9d.	6d. to 7d.
Sugar	lb.		5½d.	9d. to 10d.	6d. to 8d.	10d.	8d. to 10d.
Treacle	lb.	5½d.	4d.	5½d.		7d.	4½d.
Beef	lb.	6d. to 7d.		5d.	9d.	8d.	8½d.
Mutton	lb.	6d. to 7d.		5d.	9d.	8d.	9d.
Pork	lb.	6d. to 7d.		3½d. to 4½d.	10½d.		9½d.
Bacon	lb.			7d.			10d. to 1s. 0d.
Candles	lb.	9½d.	9d.	8½d.		9d.	9d.
Salt	lb.		1½d.	3d.			
Soap	lb.		8½d.	9d.		9½d.	8d.

[1] Prices for 1798 are from the Sutton Poor House account; all other prices are from W. Rowbottom, 'Chronology or Annals of Oldham' (MSS.).

nearly every one of their employees in the mill. The quantity is not stated, but the charge was usually 6s. 9d., and as potatoes averaged 6s. a load at the end of the year, the 6s. 9d. paid in March was probably for a load. In the following year when the crisis was over no payments for potatoes appear in the accounts.

The effect of the fall in prices is shown in Appendix B, Table VIII which has been constructed from information in the Burrs Mill wage book. The twelve families have been chosen at random and in every case the proportion of the income spent at the shop is much smaller during January to June, 1802, than in the same months of the previous year. The increase in the number and value of the notes paid off indicates great prosperity—of houses better equipped and people better clothed.

CHAPTER V

STYAL, A COUNTRY FACTORY COMMUNITY

THE QUARRY BANK MILL

IT WAS twelve years or so after Arkwright had obtained his patent for spinning cotton by rollers that Samuel Greg, one of the younger members of the large family of a Belfast shipowner, was invited by his mother's family (who lived in Ardwick) to come to England with a view to starting cotton spinning with their assistance. He accepted the invitation and came to Manchester, where he soon realized the possibilities in the new industry, and determined to set up in business for himself. After exploring Lancashire, Derbyshire and Cheshire in search of a favourable place for his venture, he finally selected a site below the junction of the Bollin and Dean at Styal, nine miles south of Manchester.

The exact date at which Samuel Greg left Belfast and the length of time it took to build the mill are uncertain. But it is known that the factory began working in 1784, cost £16,000 to erect, and, according to Greg's own statement, nearly ruined him. The bulk of the yarn produced was sold in Manchester for the home market, but some yarn was put out among the handloom weavers at Eyam in Derbyshire, where the cloth woven was a mixture of linen and cotton. Despite the fact that the machinery installed proved to be of inferior quality, the business prospered, and in 1796 Peter Ewart (who had erected one of the first engines to drive cotton machinery, at Drinkwater's factory in Manchester about 1789) was taken into partnership by Greg.[1] To this partnership Ewart, the Greg records tell us, 'brought no capital but extensive mechanical knowledge'. He seems to have been responsible for great alterations and extensions of the factory, and within a few years a new wing was built, the roof was raised and a new storey constructed; a second water wheel made of iron (the first used in the country) was installed; and, in 1800, a 10-horse-power engine was put down and some water frames of an improved type were added to the existing plant. By 1815 there were 4,416 spindles at work.

Samuel Greg does not appear to have suffered severely from the post-war depression, for, in 1818, he began extensive improvements which included the making of a tunnel and a wheelrace, an addition to the mill, and more new machinery. The cost of this extension, according to the records, was as follows:

	£
Tunnel and wheelrace	5,000
Water wheel	2,300
Mill extension	2,700
Water frames, at 12s. 3d. a spindle	1,764
	£11,764

[1] The partnership lasted five years; later Peter Ewart started in business for himself in Peter Street, Manchester, as a mule spinner. For further information about Peter Ewart (1767–1842) and the early cotton industry, see A. E. Musson and E. Robinson, 'Science and industry in the late eighteenth century', *Economic History Review*, 2nd. Ser., Vol. XIII, No. 2, December, 1960, p. 229, and W. H. Chaloner, 'Robert Owen, Peter Drinkwater and the early factory system in Manchester', *Bulletin of the John Rylands Library*, Vol. XXXVII, No. 1, September, 1954, p. 97, n. 2.

This was the last big change at Quarry Bank during times of prosperity. The place could not be expanded on a big scale and it was considered inadvisable to build another mill in a situation where it was so difficult to obtain labour. Hence subsequent developments were made in other districts; and between 1823 and 1833 Greg and his sons acquired mills at Bury, Lancaster, Caton (near Lancaster) and Bollington.[1]

After the collapse of 1825–1826 the Styal business suffered severely. Greg resisted the introduction of the power-loom weaving by means of which his fellow spinners were retrieving their losses. The balance sheets of the firm from 1825 to 1838 give ample proof of the losses on spinning certain counts and the necessity for combining spinning with weaving if a continuance of these were to be avoided. In 1834 Samuel Greg died, and the following year power-looms were installed. The cloth manufactured was still 'union', a mixture of linen weft and cotton warp. Later, however, yarn for weft was bought in Manchester and cloth entirely of cotton was manufactured. In 1838 a new weaving shed was built, and mules were bought from Sharp and Roberts so that the yarn for weft could be spun in the mill. These changes were beneficial, and from 1840 onwards the concern, though not immune from changes of fortune, was generally prosperous.

THE STYAL COMMUNITY

Having built his mill in a place with a very scanty population Greg had to obtain the workers he required from other places. The labour imported into the mill was of three types: (a) apprentices taken from the workhouses (no children younger than nine years were ever employed at this mill) who were housed, clothed and fed, but who received no wages; (b) apprentices, who were engaged by a contract made direct with their parents, and who were housed and fed (but not clothed) and paid a small weekly wage ranging from 9d. to 1s. 6d.; (c) free labour, much of which was obtained through Cheshire overseers and taken from Buckinghamshire and Berkshire through the Poor Law Commissioners.

Greg had also to provide for the needs of the families he persuaded to settle at Styal. To do this he built cottages, or bought farms and made them into cottages, and opened a shop, which, judging from the bewildering variety of commodities stocked, was a forerunner of Harrods. As the colony increased in size, a farm was bought which supplied the work-people with milk, butter and other farm produce. In 1822 a chapel was built—many of the operatives were Baptists—and a minister was engaged at a stipend of £80 a year. The following year an institution for lectures and social functions and a school were erected at Styal.

The shop accounts cover the period 1823–1828 and tell us the goods purchased for the shop, the general running expenses, the sales, and profits. The farm book contains the amounts of milk and butter sold to the villagers every day from 1825 to 1831. The Apprentice House accounts relate to the years 1823–1828 and give the cost of maintaining the apprentices.

There is little evidence as to the cost of living at Styal, but plenty of evidence as to the kind of food eaten by the workers' families. Flour, meal, potatoes, bacon, a little fresh meat, cheese and large quantities of skimmed milk were the staple foodstuffs sold to the operatives and their families. The better-off families always had new milk (at 2d. a quart) and butter

1 *Select Committee on Manufactures, Commerce, and Shipping*, 1833, p. 675.

(at 1s. 4d. a pound), and nearly all families had at least half-a-pound of butter a week in days of prosperity; but in the hard times of the late '20s butter became a luxury beyond the means of all but men earning the highest wages; even the consumption of skimmed milk, at 1d. a quart, had to be cut down.[1] Buttermilk, the demand for which remained fairly constant, was sold at ½d. a quart.

The only articles for which prices are given are new, skimmed, and sour milk, cream and butter, which, as one would expect in an agricultural district, were sold at prices considerably below town prices. This would probably be the same in the case of all farm produce, such as bacon, cheese and vegetables. The prices paid for the other commodities would, of course, depend on the way in which the Gregs took advantage of their monopoly of sale.[2]

The shop accounts afford us a glimpse of human nature which shows how quickly an increase of income is reflected in the attire of the women and girls. There are no wage books for the '20s, but it is probable that wages were increased through overtime. Before 1825 the shop stocked pattens, or clogs, and shawls for its women customers, but during 1825 hats and shoes figure in the accounts; £21 7s. 3d. was laid out on millinery, and 'plate' hats were evidently fashionable in Styal. The boom in hats did not last long, for declining trade checked the spread of the new fashions; only about £10 was expended on hats in 1826, and still less in the next two years, and clogs once more became the principal footwear.

To be just to the women it must be added that they took advantage of the period of prosperity to replenish their household goods generally, and a brisk trade was done in blankets, calico, cambric, stockings, underclothing and clothing of all kinds. The shop laid out £318 16s. 9d. on these goods in 1824, £490 13s. 7d. in 1825, but only £314 3s. 6d. in 1827.

[1] The quantities of milk and butter sold during the years 1825–1831 show the effect of hard times:

Week Ending	No. of Customers	Milk (quarts)			Butter (lb.)
		New	Skimmed	Buttermilk	
April 16, 1825 .	79	12½	1,003	109	70
April 15, 1826 .	87	21½	1,095	106	94½
April 12, 1827 .	86	15½	1,148	102	60½
April 14, 1828 .	83	35½	830½	89	58
April 19, 1829 .	86	15	770	90	53
April 17, 1830 .	81	35	837	147	48½
February 26, 1831	70	44½	545	94½	26½

The Baptist minister was responsible for the sudden increase in the sale of new milk in 1826. The previous year he bought only skimmed milk; in 1829 he returned to the more economical article.

[2] The shop's accounts were balanced and the net profits declared every six months. Profits on sales during the years 1823–1828 were as follows:

		Sales £	Profits £
1823	March–August . .	1,248	165
1824	September–February	1,433	197
	March–August . .	1,548	109
1825	September–February	1,711	230
	February–August .	1,800	107
1826	September–February	1,931	283
	March–September .	1,641	321
1827	September–March . Accounts not made up		
	March–September .	1,767	270
1828	September–March .	1,507	186

Judging from the shop sales it would appear that no serious privations were suffered up to the middle of 1828. In 1829, however, the position became more serious, as has already been indicated in the account of the sale of dairy produce.

The debt cash book covers the years 1828–1841, and gives many glimpses of the characters of the borrowers. There are shiftless people who borrowed to pay off bills which had been run up at the shop (the operatives not always being as prompt with their payments as the book-keeper had been with the deductions under the older system), and thrifty people who borrowed to buy pigs, which they later sold to the shop as bacon. Many persons borrowed money to buy clothing, and some for the funerals of relatives (the mill operatives had a funeral club). In short, money was borrowed for any transaction the negotiation of which was beyond the surplus of a weekly wage. The amounts lent varied from £1 to £20, the latter sum appearing, however, only on very rare occasions. Indeed, the majority of loans were of small sums which were paid off at a rate of from 1s. to 5s. a week.

Labour and Earnings

From the wage books it has been possible to compile tables showing the numbers, occupations and earnings of the workers in 1790, 1831 and 1848.

In February, 1790, there were 183 free labourers and eighty apprentices employed at the factory. These 183 wage-earners were distributed as shown in Table X:

TABLE X

Distribution of 183 Wage-Earners at Styal, February, 1790

Spinning rooms .	56	Labourers . .	8
Carding rooms .	77	Smiths . . .	3
Reelers . . .	22	Joiners . . .	2
Packers . . .	4	Clockmakers .	7
Roller coverers .	2	Turners . . .	2

The wages they earned were:

Carding rooms	s.	d.	s.	d.
Overlooker	15	0	—	
Head carders	9	0 to 11	9	
Carders	4	0 to 5	0	
Creel tenters	1	6 to 3	0	

Spinning rooms	s.	d.	s.	d.
Overlookers	12	6 to 13	0	
Spinners	4	0 to 5	6	
Learners	2	6 to 3	0	
Doffers	1	6	—	
Reelers	4	6 to 4	9	

Miscellaneous	s.	d.	s.	d.
Packers	9	0 to 10	0	
Clockmakers	14	0 to 25	0	
Turners	15	0 to 19	0	
Joiners	12	0 to 17	0	
Smiths	13	0 to 14	0	
Labourers	9	0 to 10	0	

These wages are time-rates for a twelve-hour day: as trade was good in 1790 longer hours were worked and overtime was paid. Even the apprentices were paid something when they worked more than twelve hours a day, for each week there are long lists of payments to apprentices of sums ranging from 3d. to 1s.

By 1831 the wage-earning workers had increased to 351 and the apprentices to 100. Wage rates were higher and there was a considerable increase in the number of adult and better-paid workers.

The Gregs had been badly hit in the panic of 1825 and the depression that followed, so it is almost certain that the improvement in wages was fairly recent. There are no wage-books for the 1820s, but the decline in purchases of clothing, milk and butter in the later years of the decade suggests that the workers shared in the reduction of wages which was general throughout the cotton industry.

Of the 351 people employed in 1831, 115 were in the carding room, eighty-seven in the spinning room: the remainder consisted of pickers, scutchers, reelers, winders, mechanics, warehousemen and labourers (Table XI).

TABLE XI

DISTRIBUTION OF 351 WAGE-EARNERS AT STYAL, 1831

	WAGES s. d.	s. d.
Scutchers	9 0 to	15 0
Boys	2 6	—
Winders:		
Overlookers	11 0	—
Winders	2 0 to	4 0
Reelers:		
Overlookers	16 0	—
Reelers	5 0 to	10 0
Carding rooms:		
Head carder	17 0 to	18 0
Carders and framers	4 6 to	10 0
Creel tenters	2 3 to	3 6
Spinning rooms:		
Overlookers	17 0 to	18 0
Spinners	6 6	—
Learners	3 6	—
Doffers	2 0 to	3 0
Warehouse:		
Adults	9 0 to	15 0
Youths	2 0 to	5 0
Mechanics:		
Adults	18 0 to	22 0
Youths	9 0	—
Odd hands	8 0 to	13 0

By February, 1848, power-loom weaving had been introduced and the apprenticeship system abandoned. The personnel of the mill was now 421 wage-earners, and the improvement of the economic position of the workers due to the introduction of power-loom weaving is shown in Table XII:

TABLE XII

EFFECT OF POWER-LOOM WEAVING ON WAGES

Wages	Numbers Employed		
	1790	1831	1848
Under 2s.	13	6	32
2s. and under 3s.	30	67	18
3s. and under 4s.	18	41	50
4s. and under 5s.	41	24	16
5s. and under 6s.	38	35	30
6s. and under 7s.	1	78	77
7s. and under 8s.	2	10	57
8s. and under 9s.	2	9	49
9s. and under 10s.	9	13	18
10s. and under 12s.	8	24	11
12s. and under 15s.	10	17	28
15s. and under 20s.	7	19	25
20s. and under 25s.	1	5	10

The source from which the Gregs drew their labour has already been indicated; the low wages they offered would not attract town labour, and therefore they communicated with parish overseers, who put them into touch with needy and suitable families. To those eking out a miserable existence with the assistance of poor relief, work in this mill meant a good house and decent food and clothing, instead of a wretched hovel, starvation and rags.[1]

[1] Dr. J. P. Kay in his report on the migration of labourers (*First Annual Report of the Poor Law Commissioners for England and Wales*, 1835, p. 201) gives the contracts of three of the families engaged through the Poor Law Commissioners by Greg & Sons:

John Howlett's Agreement: 24s. a week first year, 27s. a week second year

		s.	d.
John Howlett, employed as foreman,	aged 38	12	0
Mary Ann, factory	aged 16	4	6
Ann, factory	aged 14	3	6
Celia, factory	aged 12	2	6
Timothy, factory	aged 10	1	6
No younger children.		24	0

John Stevens' Agreement: 26s. a week first year, 29s. a week second year

		s.	d.
John Stevens, labourer	aged 38	12	0
Elizabeth, factory	aged 18	6	0
Rebeckah, factory	aged 14	3	6
James, factory	aged 12	3	0
Mary, factory.	aged 10	1	6
Five younger children.		26	0

However, the miserable circumstances from which the Gregs took some of their employees do not account for people staying in Styal once they had got their bearings in the new work and had heard of the wages offered in other districts. Probably many did move on to seek their fortunes in fields that offered greater opportunities, but, as has already been mentioned, the wage books show that some families remained in the employ of the firm generation after generation. To understand this contentment with low wages we have to remember that Styal was situated in an agricultural district where wages were low and there was little employment for women and children, and that life in Styal offered many advantages—pleasant surroundings, a good cottage and large garden, steady work, and the social ties formed by living in a small self-contained community—all of which must have weighed heavily in the balance when a move was being considered. In view of these conditions it is not difficult to account for the entire absence of trade unionism among the factory hands; very probably the more spirited members of the community migrated to other places, and those who remained in Styal acquired the placid outlook on life of their agricultural neighbours.

THE APPRENTICES

Five minutes' walk from the Quarry Bank Mill, along a pretty lane, is the Apprentice House, where for sixty-three years the indentured children employed by the firm lived. The story of the way in which some manufacturers took advantage of their power over the apprentices in their care makes one of the darkest chapters in the early history of the factory industry. The Greg family, however, took special pride in their treatment of these children. They claimed that their apprentices became healthy, respectable and industrious young people, considerably above the average of the neighbouring population. Of the boys who were receiving a few pence for working overtime in 1790, several rose to the best positions in the factory, and became overlookers, mechanics and so on. In the 1831 table, in the section dealing with family incomes, names such as Pepper, Heath, and Venables are known to be those of the families of men who were apprenticed in 1790. One of the apprentices became book-keeper to the firm, and at least two of the managers at the mill started their industrial careers as parish apprentices. These are only a few instances casually met with, and in view of the fact that the firm always kept from ninety to a hundred apprentices until they were in the process of abandoning the system, and that many hundreds of children must have

---

Hannah Veasy's Agreement: 20s. a week first year, 23s. a week second year

		s.	d.
Hannah Veasy, widow.			
Samuel, factory	aged 18	7	0
Fanny, factory	aged 16	6	0
Henry, factory	aged 14	3	6
Joseph, factory	aged 12	2	1
Mary, factory.	aged 10	1	5
		20	0

These families came from Bledlow, Bucks, where the men earned 6s. to 8s. a week and 30s. to 40s. at harvest time, averaging about 10s. a week throughout the year. Children earned from 6d. to 1s. a week in lace making and could make 4s. a week when working eight hours a day. They lived under the most miserable conditions conceivable; they had little food, their cottages had mud floors and little furniture, fires were lit only for cooking.

passed through their hands, it is impossible without a careful investigation to say whether their apprentices usually enjoyed a prosperous career. It may be said, however, that, unless the apprentices of 1790 were a very superior set of boys, there are grounds for the claims made by the firm.

Indentures show that the children were brought from all parts of the country: Newcastle-under-Lyme, Liverpool, London, and many Cheshire parishes are mentioned as their birthplaces. A description of their life as apprentices is preserved in a report[1] of the prosecution of two boys before a Middlesex magistrate, on a charge of 'having eloped and deserted the service of Samuel Greg'. The magistrate questioned them closely about their life at Styal, and was informed by them that there were forty-two boys and a larger number of girls lodged at the Apprentice House. The children were under the care of a master and mistress, the boys being accommodated on one side of the house and the girls on the other. Two apprentices shared each bed and the beds were clean and comfortable, for the sheets were changed once a month! The Apprentice House was also kept very clean, the rooms were aired every day, washed frequently and white-washed once a year. The children were given new Sunday clothes every two years, and new working clothes whenever they needed them. For breakfast and supper their food consisted of oatmeal porridge and milk, bread and milk, or milk porridge; for dinner they had boiled pork, bacon, potatoes, peas, beans and other vegetables when in season; and on Sundays there was beef, mutton or veal. Milk was the usual drink, but the apprentices were given tea when ill. Sunday mornings were spent at church, and Sunday afternoons at school; in the evenings the children were free to play. The boys also had to attend school one night a week, eight boys going each night. The runaway apprentices concluded their evidence by saying they had no complaints to make against their employer: they had left him, they said, because they wanted to see their mothers.

Evidently these were by no means the only apprentices who ran away from Quarry Bank, for many of the indentures preserved there bear a record of the conduct of the persons to whom they refer—when they ran away, where they were found, whether they were taken before magistrates, and so on. The dash for liberty was made several times by some hardy spirits, and this is not surprising, for life spent between an apprentice house and a factory, far from relatives, must have been monotonous in the extreme, even if the conditions were exceptionally good in comparison with those usually provided for children taken from overseers.

The statement of the boys about the amount of education given describes the schooling provided for apprentices as long as the system lasted. Part of the teaching was given by members of the Greg family. The daughters spent their Sunday afternoons teaching the girls, and the sons taught the boys. All the children were taught reading, writing and arithmetic; the girls were also taught to sew and were trained in housework. In the accounts for the '20s two men are mentioned as being paid small salaries for teaching at the school, and two 'singing masters' were also employed.

These parish children undoubtedly constituted cheap labour, but the accounts of the Apprentice House rather suggest the conclusion that where the employer discharged his responsibilities adequately, the labour which he housed, clothed and fed was not as cheap as free labour. Possibly these are the reasons for the rapid disappearance of the apprentice system from the cotton industry once free labour could be obtained.

[1] 'Quarry Bank Memoranda' [Greg MSS.], p. 29.

The firm made a calculation of the cost per head of the apprentices at eight different periods, and the results are interesting if only for the light they throw on the rise of the cost of living in the '40s. The weekly cost in various years was as follows:

	s.	d.		s.	d.
1790:	3	6	1840:	4	5
1822:	5	$0\frac{1}{4}$	1842:	6	$5\frac{1}{2}$
1830:	5	$0\frac{1}{2}$	1846:	9	2
1835:	4	2	1847:	13	4

The last apprentices finished their term of service in 1847, and the Apprentice House was then turned into a private dwelling.

CHAPTER VI

THE TRIUMPH OF THE FACTORY SYSTEM
AND ITS EFFECTS UPON FAMILY INCOME

IN THE 1830s economic and social questions relating to the cotton industry, and those employed in it, claimed a large measure of public interest. Attention was focussed on the industry because of the intolerable evils created by the rapid growth of the cotton manu-facturing towns, the vigorous agitation carried on against the conditions of work in factories, the acute distress among handloom weavers, and the protracted depression from which the cotton trade suffered after the collapse of 1825. With a view to devising measures to deal with these problems extensive investigations were undertaken both by the Government and by private individuals. Consequently there is a considerable body of information available from which it is possible to get a broad view of the position of the cotton workers at a time when the transition from domestic to factory production had reached a critical stage.

One of the most important investigations was undertaken by a number of Commissioners appointed by the Government in 1833 to enquire into the employment of children in factories. The Commissioners did not confine their enquiries solely to children, they also collected valuable information about all types of workers in the factory industry. The wage statistics relate solely to individual earnings and give no indication of family income but this deficiency is overcome to some extent by the details given by Dr. J. P. Kay, an Assistant Poor Law Commissioner, of the incomes of 119 families whose working members were employed by Thomas Ashton of Hyde.[1]

THE HANDLOOM WEAVERS

In the same year an investigation of the position of families dependent upon handloom weaving in thirty-five small towns and villages in North Lancashire was carried out by a number of private individuals, with the assistance of ministers, churchwardens, overseers and constables.[2] From these sources it is possible to get a fairly comprehensive view of the conditions of those workers still engaged in handloom weaving compared with those employed in various factory processes. The comparison is one of wretched poverty with one, for those times, of a measure of comfort.[3]

During the handloom weaving enquiry families were asked to state their total income and if this was below 2s. 6d. per head, particulars were taken of the size of the family, the number of workers, their earnings, the amount expended on rent, fuel and light, and the amount left for food and clothing. 8,362 families containing 49,294 persons (out of a total population of 203,349) fulfilled this condition. Of these 23,947 were employed, 2,287 unemployed and 23,060 unfit for work. The weekly wages of the workers averaged 3s. 8⅝d., which gave an

---

[1] *First Annual Report of the Poor Law Commissioners for England and Wales*, 1835, pp. 203–4.

[2] *Select Committee on Manufactures, Commerce, and Shipping*, 1833, pp. 664–7.

[3] Dr. Mitchell (*Factories Inquiry. R. Com. Supp. Rep.* Part 1, p. 41; 1834 (167), xix) states, 'The wages in the cotton factories of Lancashire are the best in England; in that country the poor's rate is lower than in any other manufacturing district'.

E

income of 1s. 9⅝d. per head and thus, when the cost of rent, fuel and light was deducted, left 1s. 3⅛d. per head for food and clothing.[1]

The men responsible for the enquiries in two of the villages were witnesses before the *Select Committee on Manufactures, Commerce, and Shipping* and their evidence is of considerable interest because in addition to making an exhaustive investigation of the state of weaving families in 1833, they had access to wage books which enabled them to give an account of the decline in weavers' wages in their respective villages and to show the effect that the decline had had in lowering the standard of living.[2]

One investigation was carried out among fustian weavers in the village of Crompton, near Oldham, by Joshua Milne, a spinner and manufacturer whose mills were situated there,[3] and another among the calico weavers of Barrowford, near Colne, by James Grimshaw, a spinner and handloom manufacturer, who himself employed a large number of the weavers he interviewed.[4] Both gave the results of their enquiries in statistical form and Appendix B, Table IX, has been drawn up to show the position of weavers in these two branches of the manufacture in each year from 1814 to 1833.

The family Grimshaw considered typical consisted of six persons—a man, his wife and four children, three of whom were weavers. Two weavers were supposed to produce jointly as much as the man. The winding was done in the family. Grimshaw, who had an intimate knowledge of the life of handloom weavers, stated that the plainest food necessary for the maintenance of such a family was 25¼ lb. of oatmeal, or 17 lb. of oatmeal and 8¼ lb. of flour, 20 lb. of potatoes, 2 lb. of bacon, 35 quarts of blue milk, and a shillingsworth of coffee, tea, sugar and treacle.[5] He obtained the prices for these goods from 1814 to 1833 from local shopkeepers. In the table, the average cost per week of this food each year has been subtracted from the income of the family (after the cost of rent, fuel, light and repair of looms has been deducted). Thus the amount left over would be what remained for the purchase of clothes, household goods, and better food.

The statistics for the whole of the district surveyed show the depths of poverty reached by the weavers in these small manufacturing villages by 1833. Unfortunately, no particulars are given as to the condition of their houses but it does not need a great deal of imagination to picture homes where hunger was the common experience.

Joshua Milne's figures show that the Crompton handloom weavers experienced a steady decline in the net sum available to them for food and clothing during the period under consideration. Milne stated in his evidence that many of the people he interviewed were obviously unfit for work through lack of proper nourishment.[6] He did not say anything about the condition of their clothes and household possessions, but it is significant that he immediately got up a public subscription and bought 'blankets and other coarse clothing' which were distributed amongst 903 persons, most of whom were fustian weavers and their dependents.[7]

---

[1] *Select Committee on Manufactures, Commerce, and Shipping*, 1833, pp. 664, 666–7.
[2] *Loc. cit.*
[3] *Ibid.*, pp. 647–66.
[4] *Ibid.*, pp. 600–9.
[5] *Ibid.*, pp. 606.
[6] *Ibid.*, pp. 662–3.
[7] *Ibid.*, p. 663. 'We never admitted any into our books whose earnings would average more than 2s. 6d. [gross] per head per week to each family.'

These enquiries were made at the end of a long period of depression and, if the facts collected by Milne and Grimshaw are typical of the thirty-five townships investigated, the position of the handloom weavers was hopeless from the time of the collapse of 1825. For eight years they must have had a struggle to keep body and soul together and, even if they had not sold their household goods to obtain food, their houses must have been nearly destitute through their being unable to replace things worn out by the wear and tear of these years.

To understand why such a large number of people lived in miserable poverty for so long we have to remember the severity of the check the cotton industry received in 1825. The state of trade prevented, for many years, that expansion of the industry which turned handloom weaving villages into factory towns and created a great demand for labour in the manufacturing centres. The movement which took place at this time sealed the fate of the handloom weavers. The bad trade accelerated the introduction of the power loom as spinners, in order to make their businesses more profitable, added power looms to their spinning machinery and employed young women and lads as weavers. In the factory districts, however, where this movement proceeded on a large scale, children had not been brought up to a decaying industry and the handloom weavers soon became absorbed in factory employment. It was the weavers far from the factory centres, who struggled to compete with the power loom because there was no other employment open to them, who suffered most severely.[1]

At Crompton, Milne found the handloom weavers whose children were not usually employed in factories very anxious to get them there. They were also anxious to obtain employment themselves in the mills but this was difficult because those round about were already supplied with labour.[2] James Grimshaw stated that the number of handloom weavers in Barrowford had actually increased, although wages had been so low for years that no one would have entered the occupation by choice. But as no other employment was obtainable, parents, anxious to increase the pittance on which they had to maintain their families, put their children to weaving immediately it was physically possible for them to manage a loom.[3]

THE FACTORY OPERATIVES

In comparison with this evidence of widespread destitution the statistics collected by the Factory Commissioners in the early 1830s make cheerful reading. They show that the majority of the factory operatives were in receipt of wages which brought within their reach a fairly abundant diet of plain food and, if careful and thrifty, tidy clothes and decent household goods.

---

[1] The number of power looms in England increased from 12,150 in 1820 to 85,009 in 1833 (S. J. Chapman, *The Lancashire Cotton Industry*, Manchester, 1904, p. 28). Thomas Ashton, speaking of Hyde and district in 1824, stated that there was then taking place a gradual transfer of men from hand- to power-looms but since trade was expanding rapidly there was no unemployment amongst the former handloom weavers. Power-loom weavers earned 'fully one-third more'; men engaged in dressing (preparing looms) earned 24s. to 30s. a week as did overlookers. Women and boys employed as weavers earned 12s. to 14s. a week; few men undertook this type of work (*Fourth Report from Select Committee on Artizans and Machinery*, 1824, p. 314).

[2] *Select Committee on Manufactures, Commerce, and Shipping*, 1833, p. 666.

[3] *Ibid.*, p. 608.

The returns do not, of course, include all the workers employed in the factories but sufficient were obtained to allow them to be taken as representative of the various manufacturing centres. A series of tables compiled from these returns by a Manchester accountant, Samuel Stanway, were published in the report of the Commissioners.[1] The purpose of the tables was to show the proportion and sex of young children employed in cotton mills, whether they were in the employ of the master or of an operative, and the number of hours they worked.

Stanway's results are in such detail that it is hardly possible to reproduce them in full. Three of his tables are, however, of especial interest and are set out with slight modifications. Appendix B, Table X, shows the age and sex distributions of workpeople employed in various processes by masters and by operatives; Appendix B, Table XI, the age and sex distributions of persons employed at different places; and Appendix B, Table XII, the average net earnings of various types of workpeople employed at the places listed in the preceeding table.

The statistics compiled by Samuel Stanway may be supplemented by those of the incomes of 119 families employed by Thomas Ashton, spinner and power loom manufacturer of Hyde, set out by Dr. Kay.[2] Unfortunately for our purpose Thomas Ashton omitted to mention how many members in each family were in employment but if we bear in mind that only males aged over twenty-one earned more than 20s. a week,[3] that the proportion of adult males to women and children was roughly one to four,[4] and that the next highest wage was 13s. paid to 295 women weavers aged twenty-one and over, we can see that under the most favourable circumstances it must have taken the labour of several individuals to bring in an income of over 40s. a week—which seventy-five out of the 119 families received. Of course, among 119 families containing 835 persons, the number of non-working members in each family varied considerably and hence the income of families of six ranged from £1 6s. 8d. to £4 10s., and of families of eight from £1 10s. to £6 5s.[5] The families with the small incomes were probably those passing through the difficult period when the children were too young to earn. In a few years their position would have improved through children entering the mill and the increased earnings of others, as was the case with the families employed at Burrs Mill thirty years earlier.

Glowing reports were given in contemporary writings of the homes of Thomas Ashton's employees.[6] The houses were of a far superior type to the ordinary working-class dwelling. Three hundred houses built by him for his workpeople had a sitting room, kitchen, pantry, two or three bedrooms and a walled yard. The women appear to have taken a pride in these model dwellings, for the cleanliness and comfort of their homes made this factory colony an object of wonder and admiration.

There is no record of the diet of Thomas Ashton's employees but it is probable that they

[1] *Factories Inquiry. R. Com. Supp. Rep.* Part I, pp. 119–33; 1834 (167), xix.

[2] *First Annual Report of the Poor Law Commissioners for England and Wales*, 1835, pp. 203–4.

[3] 234 earned on average £1 4s. 6d. each weekly (*Ibid.*, p. 204).

[4] There were 523 males and 653 females. Of these 234 males were aged 21 and over and there were 942 women and children (*Loc. cit.*).

[5] *Ibid.*, pp. 203–4.

[6] See, for example, *First Annual Report of the Poor Law Commissioners for England and Wales*, 1835, p. 203; J. P. Kay, *op. cit.*, pp. 64–8; P. Gaskell, *Artisans and Machinery*, London, 1836, p. 294; A. Ure, *The Philosophy of Manufactures*, second edition, London, 1835, pp. 348–51.

enjoyed more satisfactory food than appears to have been customary among the factory operatives at this time. There were, of course, more facilities for preparing meals in these kitchens than in the wretched hovels inhabited by many of the workers in manufacturing towns, but still more important was the fact that Ashton did not encourage the employment of married women in his mills. This alone suggests that the Hyde families kept a better table than was possible in homes where the housewife spent her days in the mill.

There is no doubt that the combination of good wages, decent houses and houseproud women showed beneficial results in improving the standard of living, for enquirers as biased in favour of the factory system as Dr. Ure, and as unbiased as Dr. Kay, tell the same story of well-furnished clean houses and healthy people.[1]

Nor was progress confined solely to material things. The working classes of Hyde seem to have profited by the education provided by Thomas Ashton and others, and to have developed a degree of culture superior to that of the average cotton operative. Possibly a partial explanation of this lay in the fact that the Ashtons were Unitarians and Hyde a strong Unitarian centre in the 1830s. But, whatever the reason, Hyde was certainly the most progressive of the new cotton manufacturing towns.

The conditions of the factory workers and their families in Manchester at this time forms a sharp contrast to this picture of humble prosperity. In an earlier chapter[2] we saw something of the conditions under which the working classes of Manchester were living at the end of the eighteenth century: by the 1830s their conditions were immeasurably worse. In the early years of the century the population of Manchester had increased more rapidly than that of any other town in England. Large numbers of people had come in, attracted by the prospect of obtaining employment in the new occupations. There was no adequate accommodation for this constant flow of newcomers and consequently the working-class districts were hopelessly congested. The town grew with phenomenal rapidity and in the absence of building regulations the multitudes of badly constructed cottages, erected without the slightest regard for health or convenience, became vast slums.[3]

The squalor which increased unchecked had undoubtedly a great influence upon the characters of the cotton workers and their families. Long working hours and sordid surroundings did not improve people whose habits were rough to begin with and made it difficult for those possessing more refinement not to descend to the level of their neighbours. Whether justifiable or not, there seems to have been a unanimous opinion that the factory workers of Manchester at this time had gross habits, lived in dirty and ill-furnished houses and ate the coarsest of food.[4]

[1] See above, p. 50.

[2] Chapter III, pp. 20–26.

[3] In 1803 the Manchester Board of Health reported, 'The number of large Cotton manufactories lately erected, the introduction of other branches of manufacture by machinery, and the consequent increase of inhabitants, without adequate increase of dwellings for their reception, cannot fail to inspire apprehensions in those who have watched the progress of sickness and mortality in former years' (*Proceedings of the Board of Health in Manchester*, Manchester and London, 1805, pp. 242–3). And in 1825 it observed that, 'The rapid increase of the population—the number of narrow, ill-ventilated, unpaved, unscavenged, and most filthy streets, that weekly rise around us, many of which are almost immediately filled by new settlers from the sister-kingdom of Ireland, who usually arrive in a state of utmost destitution, and not infrequently bring the disease of Fever with them, and are removed to the House of Recovery within a week or fortnight of their arrival in the town. . .' (Preface to *The Report of the Board of Health in Manchester*, Manchester, 1825).

[4] P. Gaskell, *op. cit.*, p. 363 et seq; H. Gaulter, *The Origin and Progress of the Malignant Cholera in Manchester*, London, 1833, passim; J. P. Kay, *op. cit.*, passim.

To picture the kind of life they lived it is sufficient to say that many working-class families lived in back-to-back two-roomed houses, situated in courts, or in badly sewered or unsewered streets, not infrequently littered with garbage and made hideous by cesspools.[1] In addition they were unable to obtain adequate supplies of water. Under these conditions it is not difficult to realize why the standard of life of the majority of the Manchester operatives was so low and why many public-spirited individuals regarded with abhorrence the factory system, which they believed to be responsible for the degradation of the work-people. Certainly surroundings such as these were not conducive to the physical and moral progress of the heterogenous collection of people who drifted into the town from the country districts round about, from places further afield, and from Ireland.

Dr. Kay, who made a close study of the Manchester factory operatives, attributed their wretched physique largely to the diet which, he stated, consisted of tea, bread, boiled potatoes with fried fat bacon and, occasionally, meat and spirits. The daily menu was as follows:

Breakfast (8 a.m., lasting 30–40 minutes). Tea ('almost always of a bad, and sometimes of a deleterious quality, the infusion is weak, and little or no milk is added') or coffee with a little bread. Sometimes men had oatmeal porridge 'but the stimulus of tea is preferred, and especially by the women'.

Dinner (noon, lasting one hour). Boiled potatoes with melted lard and butter. A 'few pieces of fried fat bacon are sometimes mingled with them, and but seldom a little meat'. The better off 'add a greater proportion of animal food . . . at least three times in a week; but the quantity consumed by the labouring population is not great'.

Supper (7 or 8 p.m.). Tea, often mingled with spirits, and a little bread. Sometimes oatmeal or potatoes.[2]

---

[1] In 1832 the Manchester Board of Health made a survey of certain parts of the town. In the fourteen districts investigated, 687 streets were inspected: of these 248 contained heaps of refuse, deep ruts, stagnant pools, ordure, etc. (J. P. Kay, *op. cit.*, p. 17).

[2] J. P. Kay, *op. cit.*, pp. 8–9. This description is corroborated by the evidence of the wife of a Manchester fine spinner before the Factory Commissioners in 1833. Breakfast consisted of porridge or bread and milk, lined with flour or oatmeal on weekdays and tea, bread and butter on Sundays. Potatoes, bacon and bread (usually white) were provided for dinner on weekdays and a little fresh meat but 'no butter, egg, or pudding' on Sundays. Supper on weekdays consisted of oatmeal porridge and milk, sometimes potatoes and milk. On Sundays (but never on weekdays) a little bread and cheese was sometimes provided. When eggs fell to ½d. each the spinner's wife occasionally fried some with bacon. The weekly order for husband, wife and five children consisted of:

	s.	d.
1½ lb. butter	1	3
1½ oz. tea	0	4½
Bread baked at home	4	6
¼ peck oatmeal	0	6½
1½ lb. bacon	0	9
40 lb. potatoes	1	4
7 quarts milk	1	9
1 lb. meat (Sundays)	0	7
1½ lb. sugar	0	9
Pepper, mustard, salt, etc.	0	3
Soap and candles	1	0
Coals	1	6
Rent	3	6
Total	18	1

The fine spinner gave his wife 25s. a week. There was thus 6s. 11d. left for clothing, sickness, schooling and miscellaneous items (*Factories Inquiry. R. Com. 1st Rep.*, Section D1, pp. 39–40; 1833 (450), xx.)

It should be added that mule spinners did not, as a rule, live on this meagre fare. The most severe critics of the way of life of the factory workers admitted that they formed a class apart from the ordinary mill hands and had a much higher standard of living.

In the writings of the period the Irish population of the towns are very frequently blamed for the wretched example they set to those among whom they settled. Accustomed as they were to a miserable standard of living it is generally agreed that, for a considerable time, their increased earnings in English manufacturing towns had no marked effect upon their way of life.[1] If this belief is well founded, the factory workers must certainly have suffered from contact with them, for there was a considerable proportion of Irish in the Manchester cotton mills, chiefly in the preparation rooms.[2]

However, it hardly seems necessary to look so far afield for an explanation of the low standard of living of the Manchester operatives. The standard of living of a family, given a certain income, depends almost entirely upon the character and capacity of the woman, and in the wretched dwellings of the working-class districts there can have been little to encourage women to cultivate domestic qualities. In this way the ignorance and incapacity of the women tended to intensify the squalor of their homes. The factory must almost have been a refuge from many of these homes and this is perhaps a reason why married women went out to work even when their husband's incomes were sufficient to maintain the family. Under such circumstances the bread and potato diet, which Dr. Kay said was general, is not surprising. When factory women did obtain help with their domestic duties it usually consisted of a child too young, or a woman too infirm, to work—neither of whom was likely to produce well-cooked meals.

Although in Manchester the private lives of the people were not interfered with as they were in some cotton manufacturing districts, yet conditions were so bad that it is not too much to say that in the Manchester of the 1830s we see the Industrial Revolution at its ugliest. The forces which were, to some extent, to remedy this deplorable state of affairs came into operation only after the close of our period. With better conditions, the spread of education and the formation of social ties, the morale of the Manchester factory workers improved, and the differences between them and the factory workers in the smaller cotton towns became much less.

It was in these smaller towns such as Bolton, Oldham, Stockport, Accrington and Bury, that the cotton factory workers, whose forefathers had been recruited from far and wide, developed those strong characteristics which later caused them to rank high in the hierarchy of labour.

---

[1] In *The Report of the Board of Health in Manchester*, Manchester, 1831, pp. 4–5, reference is made to an epidemic of gastro-enteritis raging in the town, the origin of which lay 'partly in the poverty of diet, in the habits of intemperance, in the alteration of exciting and depressing passions, in the want of personal cleanliness, and in the impure air generated in filthy back-streets, lanes, alleys, and courts of the town, and in the miserable, dark, and ill-ventilated hovels of the poorer classes, more especially those of Irish labourers, in which six, eight, ten, twelve and even fourteen persons, are sometimes found occupying, nightly as well as daily, the same room. . . . Irish labourers more particularly, appear to possess a strong antipathy against cleanliness and fresh air in their habitations. . . . The unhappy occupants of these dens of filth, with their squalid complexions, sunken eyes, and languid movements, have their nerves rendered by habit nearly insensible to the horrible stench that prevails within them'.

[2] Unfavourable accounts of the condition of the Irish population are to be found in the Preface to *The Report of the Board of Health in Manchester*, 1825; J. P. Kay, *op. cit.*, p. 21; *Factories Inquiry. R. Com. Supp. Rep.* Part 1, Section D2, p. 204; 1834 (167), xix; *First Annual Report of the Poor Law Commissioners for England and Wales*, 1835, pp. 185–6. For more favourable references see Index to *Select Committee on Manufactures, Commerce, and Shipping*, 1833, under heading 'Irish Labourers and Operatives'.

APPENDIX A

(Supplementary to Chapter IV)

EXAMPLES OF EARNINGS AND INDENTURES AT SAMUEL GREG'S MILL AT STYAL, CHESHIRE
1790, 1831 AND 1848

EXAMPLES OF EARNINGS AT STYAL

1790   Eight Weeks January 23 to March 20

Family	No. of Workers	Sex and Probable Age	Occupation	Average Weekly Income
				£ s. d.
Brierley . .	Eight .	Two men, two women, four children	Packer, labourer, women and children carding	2 0 6
Armitt . .	Five .	Man, youth, girl, two children	Smith, winder, youth, girl and child carding	1 8 1
Swan . . .	Four .	Man, three children . . .	Head carder, children in carding room	0 18 2
Massey . .	Four .	Man, two women, girl . .	Roller coverer, spinners, girl in spinning room	1 4 3
Richardson .	Four .	Woman, youth, two children	All in carding room . . .	0 12 6½
Leigh . . .	Four .	Woman, girl, boy, child .	Reeler, others in carding room.	0 15 8½
Craven . .	Four .	Man, youth, two women .	Labourer, spinners . . .	1 0 11½
Swayne . .	Three .	Man, two children . . .	Frame cleaner, doffers . .	0 16 4½
Gallimore .	Three .	Woman, girl, child . . .	Reeler, winders	0 12 8½
Hayman . .	Three .	Two women, girl . . .	Spinners	0 13 7½

1831   Eight Weeks May to June 25

Family	No. of Workers	Sex and Probable Age	Occupation	Average Weekly Income
Bailey . . .	Nine .	Man, two youths, four women, two children	Odd hand, two saddlers, two spinners, carder, reeler, two winders	2 16 4
Johnson . .	Seven .	Man, three women, youth, two children	Maker up, winder, others in carding room	1 18 10
Venables . .	Six .	Man, two youths, two women, boy	Mechanic, maker up, picker, two spinners, winder, carding room	1 15 11
Gleave. . .	Five .	Man, woman, three children	Overlooker of carding room, picker, children in carding room	1 10 11½
Leigh . . .	Five .	Woman, youth, two girls, child	Picker, others in carding room	0 18 0
Pepper. . .	Four .	Two men, two women . .	Mechanic, carder, spinner, reeler	1 19 1
Coppack . .	Four .	Two women, two youths .	Odd hand, reeler, carding room	1 2 6
Tongue . .	Three .	Man, two women . . .	Overlooker, reeling room, reeler, picker	1 9 6
Heath . . .	Three .	Man, two children . . .	Overlooker of spinning room, doffers	1 13 4½
Goodier . .	Three .	Woman, two youths . .	Spinner, carding room . .	0 17 9

1848   Eight Weeks February to March

Family	No. of Workers	Sex and Probable Age	Occupation	Average Weekly Income
				£ s. d.
Bower . . .	Seven .	Man, four women, two youths	Five weavers, youths on mules	2 16 1½
Ollier . . .	Five .	Man, two women, two children	Odd hand, two spinners, winder, child in card room	1 10 0
Steevens . .	Five .	Two women, two youths, girl	Two weavers, reeler, winder, mule spinner	1 5 7½
Witney . .	Five .	Man, youth, three women .	Two spinners, three weavers	2 0 6½
Spromson .	Five .	Two men, three women .	Weavers	2 13 9½
Hatch . . .	Four .	Two women, girl, child . .	Two weavers, winder, girl in warehouse	0 19 10½
Revitt . . .	Four .	Man, youth, woman, child .	Odd hand, scutcher, winder, carder	1 3 6½
Morrall . .	Four .	Two men, two women . .	Mechanic, warehouseman, two weavers	2 8 4
Worthington .	Four .	Man, woman, girl, child. .	Scutcher, spinner, cardhand, winder	1 2 6

INDENTURES AT STYAL

No. 21.

BE IT REMEMBERED, It is this Day agreed by and between *Saml Greg* of *Manchester*, in the County of *Lancaster, Cotton Manufacturer* of the one Part, and *Thomas Smith, Hatters*, of *Heaton Norris in the County of Lancaster* of the other Part, as follows, That the said *Thos Smith Agreeath that Esther and Ann Smith* shall serve the said *Saml Greg* in his Cotton-Mills, in *Styall* as a just and honest Servant, *Thirteen* Hours in each of the six working Days, and to be at *theair* own Liberty at all other Times; the Commencement of the Hours to be fixed from Time to Time by the said *Saml Greg* for the Term of *Three* Years at the Wages of *one Penney per Week and Sufficient Meat Drink and Apparell Lodging washing and all other Things necessary and fit for a Servant.*

And that if the said *Esr and Ann Smith* shall absent *themselves* from the Service of the said *Saml Greg* in the said working Hours, during the said Term, that the said *Saml Greg* may not only abate the Wages proportionably, but also for the Damages sustained by such Absence. And that the said *Saml Greg* shall be at Liberty, during the Term, to discharge the Servant from his Service, for Misbehaviour, or want of Employ.

As Witness their Hands, this *Twenty Eight* Day of *Jany 1788*—

Witness   *By me Thomas Smith*

  Mattw Fawkner

BE IT REMEMBERED, IT is this Day agreed by and between SAMUEL GREG, of Styal, in the County of Chester, of the one Part, and *Wm Chadwick* of *Styall* of the other Part, as follows: That the said *Wm Chadwick* shall serve the said Samuel Greg in his Cotton-Mills, in Styal, in the County of Chester, as a just and honest Servant, *Twelve* Hours in each of the six working Days, and to be at *his* own Liberty at all other Times; the Commencement of the Hours to be fixed from Time to Time by the said Samuel Greg, for the Term of *one* Year at the Wages of *foureteen Shillings per Week.*

And that if the said *Wm Chadwick* shall absent *him self* from the Service of the said Samuel Greg, in the said working Hours, during the said Term, without his Consent first obtained, that the said Samuel Greg may abate the Wages in a double Proportion for such Absence; and the said Samuel Greg shall be at Liberty, during the Term, to discharge the Servant from his Service, for Misbehaviour, or Want of Employ.

As witness their Hands, this *fiveth* Day of *Feby 1791.*

Witness   *William Chadwick*
   Mattw Fawkner

Styall

28th Day of Octbr 1794

By this Indenture I Bind my-self to pay unto Matthw Fawkner of Styall the sum of five Pounds Elevin Shillings upon Demand and allso Asign Over my Household goods under Mentioned unto the aforesaid Matthw Fawkner till the afore said sum of five Pounds 11s. is Paid and allso allow him to sell them or any Part of them for the payment of the afforesaid money and all Expenses attending such Sale of my goods—

William Chadwick

one Chest	14/-	Bed Clothes	28/-
one Iron Pot	2/-	Fork.	1/11
one Clock	21/-	Spade	1/4
1 Bed Stocks	9/-	Shuffill	1/-
1 Do Do	—	Hatchat	2/-
7 Chairs	12/-	Mugs	2/6
Bellis	2/-	Tin Kettle	1/-
1 Pair Bed Stocks	2/6	Potts and Mugs	5/-
Iron and Heater	5/6	Cubbord	8/-
3 Small Glass		Map.	2/6
Pictures.	-/6	Little Stand	1/9
one Map	1/8	Iron Pott	5/-
Table	6/-	Sheets	8/-
one Stand	1/6	Blankets	10/-
Grate and Tongs	11/6	Copper Kettel	2/6
Frying Pann	1/4	Sundry Things	1/4

William Chadwick

APPENDIX B

STATISTICAL TABLES

B/I   The Prices Obtained for One Pound of 40 Hanks Cop Weft, the Cost of Cotton and the Sum Left for Labour, Expenses and Profit, 1815–1832.

B/II   Prices and Costs of Calico, 1814–1832.

B/III   Weekly Earnings in Manchester, 1810–1819.

B/IV   Incomes of Five Families, 1810–1819.

B/V´   Retail Prices, 1810–1819.

B/VI   Price of Food of the Simplest Kind for a Family of Six Persons, 1810–1819.

B/VII   Weekly Incomes and Expenditures of Families Employed in the Cotton Textile Industry, 1810–1819.

B/VIII   Income and Expenditure of Families Employed at Burrs Mill, Bury, January, 1801 to June, 1802.

B/IX   Earnings and Expenditures of Calico and Fustian Weavers, 1814–1833.

B/X   Number, Age and Sex of Workpeople Employed by Masters and by Operatives at Various Places in Lancashire and Cheshire, 1833.

B/XI   Number, Age and Sex of Workpeople Employed at Various Places in Lancashire and Cheshire, 1833.

B/XII   Average Net Earnings of Operatives at Various Places in Lancashire and Cheshire, 1833.

TABLE B/I

The Prices Obtained for One Pound of 40 Hanks Cop Weft, the Cost of Cotton and the Sum Left for Labour, Expenses and Profit
1815–1832[1]

Year	Price Obtained for 1 lb. 40 hanks Cop Weft	Cost of Cotton Required (18 oz.)	Sum Left for Labour Expenses and Profit	Per cent Decline Since 1815
	s. d.	s. d.	s. d.	
1815	3 0½	1 10	1 2½	—
1816	2 7½	1 8¾	0 10¾	26
1817	2 6	1 10½	0 7½	48
1818	2 6	1 10½	0 7½	48
1819	1 10½	1 3¼	0 7¼	50
1820	1 7¼	1 1¼	0 6	60
1821	1 5¼	0 10¾	0 6½	55
1822	1 4¾	0 9	0 7¾	46
1823	1 4¾	0 9¼	0 7½	48
1824	1 3½	0 9½	0 6	60
1825	1 5½	1 1¾	0 3¾	74
1826	1 1	0 7½	0 5½	62
1827	1 0½	0 7	0 5½	62
1828	0 11¾	0 7¼	0 4½	69
1829	0 11¾	0 6½	0 5¼	63
1830	1 0¼	0 7½	0 4¾	65
1831	0 11¼	0 6½	0 4¾	65
1832	0 11¼	0 7¼	0 4	72

[1] *Select Committee on Manufactures, Commerce, and Shipping, 1833, p. 569.*

TABLE B/II

Prices and Costs of Calico, 1814–1832[1]

Year	The Average Prices at Manchester of 1 piece of Calico	Cost of Warp, Weft and Sizing	Sum Left for Labour and Profit	Average Prices Paid for Weaving 1 piece of Calico[2]
	s. d.	s. d.	s. d.	s. d.
1814	24 7	17 4½	7 2½	6 6
1815	19 8¾	14 7¼	5 1½	4 3
1816	16 8½	12 11¾	3 8¾	3 4
1817	16 1	12 2¾	3 10¼	3 0
1818	16 8½	12 7½	4 1	3 7
1819	13 9	9 11¼	3 9¾	3 1
1820	12 1½	8 2½	3 11	2 11
1821	9 8¼	6 8¾	2 11½	3 2
1822	9 3½	6 4¼	2 11¼	2 6
1823	8 11¼	6 4¼	2 7	2 4
1824	8 5¾	6 3¾	2 2	2 1
1825	8 5¼	5 11	2 6¼	2 1
1826	6 3¼	4 11	1 4¼	1 4
1827	6 6	4 9	1 9	1 7½
1828	6 5¼	4 10	1 7¼	1 7½
1829	5 8	4 10	0 10	1 2
1830	6 3¼	5 0½	1 2¾	1 6
1831	6 2¼	4 6	1 8¼	1 7½
1832	5 8	4 6	1 2	1 4

[1] The table has been constructed from information to the *Select Committee on Manufactures, Commerce, and Shipping*, 1833 (pp. 605, 607), by James Grimshaw, spinner and manufacturer of cotton at Barrowford, near Colne.

[2] 1814–1820, second seventy-four calico; 1821–1832, third seventy-four calico.

TABLE B/III

WEEKLY EARNINGS IN MANCHESTER, 1810–1819[1]

Occupation	1810		1811		1812		1813		1814		1815		1816		1817		1818		1819	
	s.	d.	s.	d.	s.	d.	s.	d.	s.	d.	s.	d.	s.	d.	s.	d.	s.	d.	s.	d.
Actual earnings of:																				
Fine spinners	42	6	18	0	30	0	27	0	32	0	32	0	32	0	32	0	32	0	32	0
Women spinners					15	7	14	2	17	0	17	0	17	0	17	0	17	0	17	0
Reelers	12	0	6	0	9	11	8	2	10	0	10	0	10	0	10	0	10	0	10	0
Stretchers	15	6	8	5	13	5	11	8	14	0	14	0	14	0	14	0	14	0	14	0
Pickers	11	3	5	6	10	1	8	8	10	0	10	0	9	0	9	0	9	0	9	0
Man weaving:																				
Nankeens	16	3	12	6	13	0	12	6	15	7	13	2	13	2	9	6	9	6	9	6
Best 74, 7–8 calicoes			9	6	11	4	12	8	13	8	10	10	9	2	8	4	9	8	8	3
Third calicoes					6	8	6	8	15	3	11	8	8	1	6	4½	8	1	6	0
Strong, 9–8 calicoes	13	0	8	9	9	7	8	9	11	4	8	9	7	4	6	1¼	7	0	7	0
Manchester Cambric, 80 reed	14	0	10	9	10	3	11	1	16	9	10	3	8	3	6	9	8	10	7	9
Quiltings, 36 reed	16	5½	12	7	9	6	11	5	15	0	13	0	11	11	9	8	9	8	9	8
Fancy articles	21	0	14	8	14	2	15	6	21	0	18	3	12	2	9	5	11	9	10	3
Average earnings for a full week's work:																				
Coarse spinners	24	0	24	0	24	0	24	0	24	0	24	0	24	0	24	0	24	0	24	0
Big piecers									10	0	10	0	10	0	10	0	10	0	10	0
Children of ten years													2	6 to	3	0				
Children of fourteen years													7	0 to	8	0				

[1] All figures are taken from G. W. Daniels, 'The Cotton Trade at the Close of the Napoleonic War', (Appendix II), *Trans. Manch. Stat. Soc.*, 1917–1918, except those of big piecers (*Minutes of Evidence before Select Committee on Manufacturers, Commerce, and Shipping*, 1833, p. 320) and of children aged 10 and 14 years (*1816 Comm.*, p. 359).

TABLE B/IV

INCOMES OF FIVE FAMILIES, 1810–1819[1]

	1810 s.	d.	1811 s.	d.	1812 s.	d.	1813 s.	d.	1814 s.	d.	1815 s.	d.	1816 s.	d.	1817 s.	d.	1818 s.	d.	1819 s.	d.
Man. Fine spinner	42	6	18	0	30	0	27	0	32	0	32	0	32	0	32	0	32	0	32	0
Child aged fourteen years . . .	7	6	4	0¾	6	10½	6	3	7	6	7	6	7	6	7	6	7	6	7	6
Child aged ten years . . .	2	9	1	6	2	6¼	2	3½	2	9	2	9	2	9	2	9	2	9	2	9
Total	52	9	23	6¾	39	4¾	35	6½	42	3	42	3	42	3	42	3	42	3	42	3
Man. Coarse spinner . . .	24	0	13	0	22	0	20	0	24	0	24	0	24	0	24	0	24	0	24	0
Child aged fourteen years . .	7	6	4	0¾	6	10½	6	3	7	6	7	6	7	6	7	6	7	6	7	6
Child aged ten years . . .	2	9	1	6	2	6¼	2	3½	2	9	2	9	2	9	2	9	2	9	2	9
Total	34	3	18	6¾	31	4¾	28	6½	33	3	33	3	33	3	33	3	33	3	33	3
Man. Weaver (Best 74, 7–8 calicoes) .			9	6	11	4	12	8	13	8	10	10	9	2	8	4	9	8	8	3
Child aged fourteen years . . .			4	0¾	6	10½	6	3	7	6	7	6	7	6	7	6	7	6	7	6
Child aged ten years . . .			1	6	2	6¼	2	3½	2	9	2	9	2	9	2	9	2	9	2	9
Total	34	3	15	0¾	20	8¾	21	2½	23	11	21	1	19	5	18	7	19	11	18	6
Man. Weaver (Manc. Cambric, 80 reed) .	14	0	10	9	10	3	11	1	16	9	10	3	8	3	6	9	8	10	7	9
Child aged fourteen years . . .	7	6	4	0¾	6	10½	6	3	7	6	7	6	7	6	7	6	7	6	7	6
Child aged ten years . . .	2	9	1	6	2	6¼	2	3½	2	9	2	9	2	9	2	9	2	9	2	9
Total	24	3	16	3¾	19	7¾	19	7½	27	0	20	6	18	6	17	0	19	1	18	0
Woman. Stretcher . . .	15	6	8	5	13	5	11	8	14	0	14	0	14	0	14	0	14	0	14	0
Child aged fourteen years . . .	7	6	4	0¾	6	10½	6	3	7	6	7	6	7	6	7	6	7	6	7	6
Child aged ten years . . .	2	9	1	6	2	6¼	2	3½	2	9	2	9	2	9	2	9	2	9	2	9
Total	25	9	13	11¾	22	9¾	20	2½	24	3	24	3	24	3	24	3	24	3	24	3

[1] Adult earnings are taken from G. W. Daniels, 'The Cotton Trade at the Close of the Napoleonic War' (Appendix II), *Trans. Manch. Stat. Soc.*, 1917–1918, and earnings of children from *1816 Comm.*, p. 359. In both cases account has been taken of the short-time known to have been worked by McConnel and Kennedy (*A Century of Fine Cotton Spinning*, p. 52).

TABLE B/V

Retail Prices, 1810–1819[1]

		1810	1811	1812	1813	1814	1815	1816	1817	1818	1819
4 lb. loaf	Highest price	1s. 5¼d. (May)	1s. 6½d. (Nov.)	1s. 8¼d. (Sept.)	1s. 6½d. (Jan./Aug.)	1s. 1¼d. (Feb./Sept.)					
	Lowest price	1s. 2¼d. (Nov.)	1s. 1¼d. (June/July)	1s. 3½d. (Feb.)	11d. (Dec.)	11½d. (Jan./July)					
Flour (12 lb., good seconds)		3s. 9d.	3s. 5d.	4s. 9d.	4s. 2d.	2s. 10d.	2s. 7d.	3s. 0d.	4s. 6d.	3s. 5d.	2s. 9d.
Meal (12 lb., good seconds)		2s. 6d.	2s. 6d.	3s. 9d.	3s. 3d.	2s. 4d.	2s. 2d.	2s. 1d.	3s. 2d.	2s. 8d.	2s. 3d.
Potatoes	20 lb.	7d. to 8d.	10d.	11d. to 22d.	9d. to 15d.	11d.	11d.	8d. to 14d.	9d. to 17d.	8½d.	8d.
Mutton	1 lb.	8d.	8d. to 9d.	7d. to 8d.	9d.	9d.	8½d.	6½d. to 7d.		6d. to 6½d.	8½d.
Pork	1 lb.	7½d. to 8d.	7½d. to 8½d.	6d. to 7d.	7½d. to 8½d.	8d. to 9d.	8d. to 9d.	4½d. to 6d.		6d. to 8d.	7½d. to 8½d.
Beef	1 lb.	8d. to 8½d.	8d. to 9d.	7d. to 9d.	8d. to 9d.	8d. to 9d.	7½d. to 8½d.	6d. to 7d.		5d. to 7d.	8d. to 8½d.
Bacon	1 lb.	11d.	9d.	10d.	11d.	11d.	10½d.	8d.	7d.	10d.	10d.
Irish butter	1 lb.	1s. 1d.	1s. 2½d.	1s. 2d.	1s. 3½d.	1s. 3½d.	1s. 2½d.	11d.	11d.	1s. 2d.	1s. 0d.
Cheese	1 lb.	8½d.	8½d.	8½d.	9d.	8½d.	8½d.	6¾d.	6¾d.	8d.	8d.
Treacle	1 lb.	5d.	5d.	6d.	6½d.	7d.	6½d.	4d. to 4½d.		5d.	5d. to 5½d.
Sugar	1 lb.	9d. to 10d.	8d. to 10d.	8d. to 10d.	8d. to 10d.	11d. to 13d.	12d. to 13d.	10d. to 13d.		9d. to 11d.	9d. to 11d.
Candles	1 lb.	1s. 0d.	10d.	11d.	1s. 0d.	13½d. to 14d.	1s. 0d.	9½d. to 10d.		10d. to 11d.	11d. to 12d.
Soap	1 lb.	11½d. to 12d.	10d. to 11d.	9d. to 10d.	10d. to 11d.	11d. to 12d.	10d. to 11d.	9d. to 11d.		10½d.	11d.

[1] The price of the 4 lb. loaf has been taken from *A Return of the Price of the Quartern Loaf of Wheaten Bread*, 1814–1815 (109) X; January prices of mutton, pork, beef, treacle, sugar, candles, soap (except for 1817 which is missing) and potatoes (1810 only) from W. Rowbottom, 'Chronology or Annals of Oldham,' and all other prices from G. W. Daniels, 'The Cotton Trade at the Close of the Napoleonic War' (Appendix II), *Trans. Manch. Stat. Soc.*, 1917–1918.

TABLE B/VI

Price of Food of the Simplest Kind for a Family of Six Persons, 1810–1819[1]

		1810	1811	1812	1813	1814	1815	1816	1817	1818	1819
		s. d.	s. d.	s. d.	s. d.	s. d.	s. d.	s. d.	s. d.	s. d.	s. d.
Flour	8½ lb.	2 8	2 0¾	3 4¼	2 11½	2 0	1 10	2 1½	3 2¼	2 0¾	1 11½
Oatmeal	17 lb.	3 6½	3 6½	5 3¾	4 7¼	3 3¾	3 1	2 11½	4 6	3 9¼	3 2¼
Potatoes	20 lb.	0 7½	0 10	1 4½	1 0	0 11	0 11	0 11	1 1	0 8½	0 8
Bacon	2 lb.	1 10	1 6	1 8	1 10	1 10	1 8	1 4	1 2	1 8	1 8
Irish butter	1 lb.	1 1	1 2½	1 2	1 3½	1 3½	1 2½	0 11	0 11	1 2	1 0
Meat	2 lb.	1 4	1 4	1 4	1 5	1 6	1 5	1 3	1 3	1 4	1 4
Cheese	2 lb.	1 5	1 5	1 5	1 6	1 5	1 5	1 1½	1 1½	1 4	1 4
Treacle	2 lb.	0 10	0 10	1 0	1 1	1 2	1 1	0 8½		0 10	0 10½
Sugar	1 lb.	0 9½	0 9	0 9	0 9	1 0	1 0½	0 11½		0 10	0 10
	Total	14 1½	13 5¾	17 4½	16 5¼	14 5¼	13 8	12 3½		13 8½	12 10¼

[1] The foodstuffs listed have been compiled by combining parts of the tables set out in Eden (*op. cit.*, Vol. II, p. 359) and in the *Select Committee of Manufactures, Commerce, and Shipping*, p. 606 (J. Grimshaw's evidence). The prices of potatoes (1810 only) and of treacle and sugar (except for 1817 which is missing) are taken from W. Rowbottom, 'Chronology or Annals of Oldham'; where two prices are recorded the mean is given. All other prices are from G. W. Daniels, 'The Cotton Trade at the Close of the Napoleonic War' (Appendix II), *Trans. Manch. Stat. Soc.*, 1917–1918.

TABLE B/VII

Weekly Incomes and Expenditures of Families Employed in the Cotton Textile Industry, 1810–1819[1]

Year	Weekly Expenditure of a Family of Six Persons	Weekly Income of Various Families				
		Fine Spinner	Coarse Spinner	Weaver (Best 74, 7–8 Calicoes)	Weaver (Manchester Cambric, 80 reed)	Woman Stretcher
	s. d.	s. d.	s. d.	s. d.	s. d.	s. d.
1810	19 10½	52 9	34 3		24 3	25 9
1811	19 2¾	23 6¾	18 6¾	15 0¾	16 3¾	13 11¾
1812	23 1½	39 4¾	31 4¾	20 8¾	19 7¾	22 9¾
1813	22 2¼	35 6½	28 6½	21 2½	19 7½	20 2½
1814	20 2¼	42 3	33 3	23 11	27 0	24 3
1815	19 5	42 3	33 3	21 1	20 6	24 3
1816	18 0½	42 3	33 3	19 5	18 6	24 3
1817	not available	42 3	33 3	18 7	17 0	24 3
1818	19 5½	42 3	33 3	19 11	19 1	24 3
1819	18 7¼	42 3	33 3	18 6	18 0	24 3

[1] Incomes are those of the families listed in Appendix B, Table IV; expenditures consist of foodstuffs (Appendix B, Table VI) plus 5s. 9d. for rent, coal and candles, soap and sundries. (See above, p. 24).

TABLE B/VIII

INCOME AND EXPENDITURE OF FAMILIES EMPLOYED AT BURRS MILL, BURY, JANUARY, 1801 TO JUNE, 1802

Family	January to June, 1801				January to June, 1802			
	Weekly Average		Total throughout Period		Weekly Average		Total throughout Period	
	Income	Shop	Cash Issued	Notes Paid Off	Income	Shop	Cash Issued	Notes Paid Off
	£ s. d.	£ s. d.	£ s. d.	£ s. d.	£ s. d.	£ s. d.	£ s. d.	£ s. d.
Crossley	1 18 0	1 5 9	0 7 8	3 2 10	2 1 4½	0 18 0	0 19 8	3 1 8½
Brooks	1 6 6	0 19 11	0 2 8	1 11 11½	2 0 2	0 15 9	0 18 6	4 15 2
Barlow	1 14 3	1 2 5	0 5 4½	5 18 8	2 0 7	0 16 6	0 16 11½	9 9 10½
Wood	1 3 11	0 11 9	0 3 4½	8 17 0	1 8 5	0 9 6	0 9 7	10 2 11
Cock	0 19 2	0 12 1	0 4 4	0 12 6	0 16 1	0 6 6½	0 5 11	1 3 10
Haworth	0 9 1	0 6 10	0 1 9	0 12 0	0 12 10	0 6 8	0 1 11½	4 10 4
Nuttall	0 16 4½	0 9 5½	0 6 2	0 5 5½	1 2 6	0 6 1½	0 13 0	2 11 5
Heap	0 12 3½	0 10 0	0 1 0	0 4 3	1 2 5½	0 8 8	0 3 11	7 12 3½
Booth	0 13 3	0 8 6	0 3 7	0 13 2	0 13 5½	0 4 7½	0 7 4	1 11 4
Wilkinson	0 16 1½	0 5 1	0 2 3½	11 16 10	0 18 9½	0 1 8½	0 4 4	14 7 3½
Chadwick	0 14 4½	0 14 2		0 2 10	0 15 4	0 11 8	0 1 6	1 5 0
Brierley	1 15 9	0 19 2	0 13 3½	1 6 0	0 16 8	0 5 10½	0 9 11	2 1 1

TABLE B/IX

Earnings and Expenditures of Calico and Fustian-Weavers, 1814–1833[1]

Year	Calico Weavers at Barrowford, near Colne					Fustian Weavers of Crompton, near Oldham		
	Average Weekly Earnings and Expenditure of a Family of Six (parents and children), Three of them Calico Weavers				Weekly Earnings of a 'Good' Calico Weaver	Weekly Earnings and Expenditures		
	Total Earnings	Earnings After Deductions of Rent, Fuel, Light and Repair of Looms[2]	Cost of Food of the Plainest Kind	Surplus After Meeting the Cost of the Plainest Food		Earnings of a 'Fair' Weaver Working 10½ hours Each Day[3]	Cost of Rent, Fuel, Light, Repair of Looms, Winding, etc.	Surplus Remaining for Food and Clothing
	s. d.	s. d.	s. d.	s. d.	s. d.	s. d.	s. d.	s. d.
1814	52 0	46 9	9 3¼	37 3¾	26 0	13 9	3 7½	10 1½
1815	34 2	28 11	8 11½	19 11½	17 1	11 9	3 3¼	8 5¾
1816	26 10	21 7	8 10½	12 8½	13 5	9 0	2 9½	6 2½
1817	24 2	18 11	12 7½	6 3½	12 1	6 6	2 4¼	4 1½
1818	28 10	23 7	10 6	13 1	14 5	8 9	2 8½	6 0½
1819	25 0	19 9	9 2	10 7	12 6	10 0	2 11	7 1
1820	23 4	18 1	9 6	8 7	11 8	9 0	2 8¾	6 3¼
1821	28 3¾	23 0¾	8 6½	14 6¼	12 7	8 6	2 7½	5 10½
1822	22 10½	17 7½	8 1	9 6	10 2	9 0	2 8¼	6 3¾
1823	21 0	15 9	9 4	7 5	9 4	9 6	2 9	6 9
1824	19 1½	13 10½	9 5½	4 5	8 6	9 6	2 8¾	6 9¼
1825	19 1½	13 10½	8 10	5 0½	8 6	8 9	2 7	6 2
1826	11 10	7 7	7 4	0 2¾	5 3	6 6	2 1½	4 4½
1827	14 7½	10 4½	9 2½	0 0½	6 6	6 6	2 2¼	4 3¾
1828	14 7½	10 4½	8 3	2 1½	6 6	7 0	2 3	4 9
1829	10 6	6 3	6 2½	0 0½	4 8	6 0	2 0¾	3 11¼
1830	13 6	9 3	9 1	0 2	6 0	5 0	1 10½	3 1½
1831	14 10	10 7	8 11½	1 7¼	6 7	5 0	1 10½	3 1½
1832	12 0	7 9	7 5	0 1¾	5 4	4 6	1 9¼	2 8¾
1833	12 0	7 9	7 9		5 4	4 6	1 9	2 9

[1] *Select Committee on Manufactures, Commerce, and Shipping*, 1833, pp. 605–6, 661.

[2] 'Indispensable' deductions during 1814–1825 and 1826–1833 came to 5s. 3d. and 4s. 3d. a week respectively.

[3] At Barrowford it has been assumed that winding was done by the family while at Crompton 2d. in each 1s. of earnings was paid for this work. The cost of winding should, therefore, be *added* to the Crompton figures in order to make them comparable with those of Barrowford (*ibid.*, p. 661n).

TABLE B/X

NUMBER, AGE AND SEX OF WORKPEOPLE EMPLOYED BY MASTERS AND BY OPERATIVES AT VARIOUS PLACES IN LANCASHIRE AND CHESHIRE, 1833[1]

Type of Employment	Adults		Persons Aged under Eighteen Years						Total Numbers Employed
			Males			Females			
	Males	Females	Employed by Masters	Employed by Operatives	Employers Uncertain	Employed by Masters	Employed by Operatives	Employers Uncertain	
Cleaners and spreaders of cotton . .	272	689	212	1	9	94	2	3	1,282
Carders	2,350	3,501	1,229	81	18	2,061	117	40	9,397
Mule spinners	5,163	1,189	697	5,852	50	346	2,284	24	15,605
Throstle spinners	194	688	373	4	32	500	4	51	1,846
Reelers	146	2,552	40	5		542	23	8	3,316
Weavers	4,627	6,108	986	610	35	2,538	1,104	32	16,040
Roller Coverers	61	87	5	1		9	7		170
Engineers, firemen, mechanics, etc. .	927	7	43	3	8	1			989
Totals	13,740	14,821	3,585	6,557	152	6,091	3,541	158	48,645

[1] *Factories Inquiry. R. Com. Supp. Rep.* Part I, p. 124; 1834 (167), xix.

TABLE B/XI

NUMBER, AGE AND SEX OF WORKPEOPLE EMPLOYED AT VARIOUS PLACES IN LANCASHIRE AND CHESHIRE, 1833[1]

Place of Employment	Persons Aged above Eighteen Years			Persons Aged above Fourteen and under Eighteen Years			Persons Aged under Fourteen Years		
	Males	Females	Total	Males	Females	Total	Males	Females	Total
Manchester and immediate neighbourhood	4,421	5,731	10,152	1,514	1,887	3,401	2,287	1,550	3,837
Stockport and Heaton Norris	2,314	2,175	4,489	583	777	1,360	973	669	1,642
Dukinfield and Stalybridge	1,251	1,256	2,507	232	163	395	320	294	614
Hyde, Brinnington, etc.	1,936	2,451	4,387	666	924	1,590	657	615	1,272
Tintwistle, Glossop, etc.	728	675	1,403	324	252	576	248	255	503
Oldham	1,318	824	2,142	371	422	793	442	398	840
Bolton	1,443	1,279	2,722	570	637	1,207	855	685	1,540
Warrington	207	235	442	53	55	108	90	76	166
Bury (one mill)	122	195	317	40	73	113	69	58	127
Totals	13,740	14,821	28,561	4,353	5,190	9,543	5,941	4,600	10,541

1 *Factories Inquiry. R. Com. Supp. Rep.* Part I, p. 124; 1834 (167), xix.

TABLE B/XII

AVERAGE NET EARNINGS OF OPERATIVES AT VARIOUS PLACES IN LANCASHIRE AND CHESHIRE, 1833[1]

Type of Employment	Age and Sex of Operatives	Number of Persons Employed	Average Number of Hours Worked During Month Ending May 4, 1833	Net Earnings of Each Worker for a 69-hour Week
				s. d.
Carders:				
Carders or overlookers	Male adults	376	275·2	23 6
Jack-frame tenters	Mainly female adults	696	273·5	8 0
Bobbin-frame tenters	Mainly female adults	945	276·8	7 5½
Drawing tenters	Mainly female adults	1,931	275·6	7 5¾
Mule spinners:				
Overlookers	Male adults	145	275·9	29 3
Spinners	Male and female adults but chiefly the former	3,797	275·5	25 8
Piecers	Male and female adults and non-adults but chiefly the latter	7,157	274·8	5 4¾
Scavengers	Male and female non-adults	1,247	272·6	2 10¾
Throstle spinners:				
Overlookers	Male adults	82	272·8	22 8½
Spinners	Female adults and non-adults	1,123	272·2	7 9
Weavers:				
Overlookers	Male adults	400	273·9	26 3½
Warpers	Male and female adults	332	273·0	12 3
Weavers	Male and female adults, male and female non-adults but chiefly females	10,171	273·7	10 9¾
Dressers	Male adults	836	276·0	27 9¾

[1] *Factories Inquiry. R. Com. Supp. Rep.* Part I, p. 124; 1834 (167), xix. For the places at which employed see previous table.

APPENDIX C[1]

WAGES IN ARKWRIGHTS' BAKEWELL MILL

DAY AND NIGHT SPINNERS

MEAN weekly numbers and earnings are extant of day and night spinners at the Arkwrights' Bakewell mill during certain quarters of 1786–1788, 1793–1796 and 1804–1811. The wage books are in the Chesterfield Public Library; a microfilm copy is in the Manchester Central Reference Library.

The wage books may be identified as those of the Bakewell mill by the references to George Harrison whose name appears in the records during the eight months ending October, 1786, when, the *Manchester Mercury* of October 17 and 31 reported, he was at Chesterfield Quarter Sessions imprisoned for six months and fined £20 for having 'kicked and otherwise abused' a child worker 'in a very unmerciful Manner, and afterwards drew it up by the Neck with a Cord. The Child was brought into Court and appeared a shocking Spectacle'. The wage books also contain the earnings of 'Youlgrave [near Bakewell] Pickers'. These were presumably outworkers.

[1] Contributed by Dr. R. S. Fitton.

TABLE C/I

MEAN WEEKLY EARNINGS OF DAY SPINNERS

Year	Quarter[1]			
	1	2	3	4
	s. d.	s. d.	s. d.	s. d.
1786	3 6¾ [2]	3 6½ [12]	3 6 [12]	3 5
1787	3 4	3 2¾	3 5½	3 4½
1788	3 4¾	3 5 [5]		
1793			3 7½ [6]	3 11¼
1794	4 1¾	3 11¾	4 0¼	4 0¾
1795	4 4½	4 1¼	4 0¾	4 0
1796	4 3¼			
1804		4 7¾ [5]	4 7¼ [11]	4 6¾ [11]
1805	5 0	4 9¾	4 11 [11]	4 8¼
1806	5 3	5 1¼	5 2 [11]	5 0 [11]
1807	5 3¾	5 1¾	5 2 [11]	5 3
1808	5 7¼	5 5½	5 5¾	5 3½
1809	5 6	5 10¼	5 9¼	5 7¼
1810	5 7¼	5 9	5 8	6 7
1811	6 5½ [11]			

[1] Where figures for complete quarters are unavailable index figures have been inserted to show the number of weeks for which the mean has been calculated.

TABLE C/II

Mean Weekly Number of Day Spinners

Year	Quarter[1]			
	1	2	3	4
1786	286 [2]	264 [12]	263 [12]	267
1787	277	273	267	270
1788	288	300 [5]		
1793			246 [6]	259
1794	265	268	268	259
1795	252	246	238	251
1796	258			
1804		225 [5]	223 [11]	226 [11]
1805	235	235	226 [11]	216
1806	212	210	196 [11]	194 [11]
1807	198	203	193 [11]	181
1808	182	186	186	186
1809	184	188	183	188
1810	198	187	194	184
1811	189 [11]			

[1] See n., p. 71.

TABLE C/III

Mean Weekly Earnings of Night Spinners

Year	Quarter[1]			
	1	2	3	4
	s. d.	s. d.	s. d.	s. d.
1786	4 1	3 10¼ [12]	4 0 [12]	3 11
1787	4 7½	4 5¼	4 4½	4 3
1788	4 1¼	4 2 [5]		
1793			5 6½ [4]	
1795	4 3 [5]	4 3½	4 7¼	4 9¼ [3]

[1] See n., p. 71.

TABLE C/IV

Mean Weekly Number of Night Spinners

Year	Quarter[1]			
	1	2	3	4
1786	60	70 [12]	59 [12]	69
1787	88	94	94	101
1788	89	61		
1793			15 [4]	
1795	20 [5]	25	27	20 [3]

[1] See n., p. 71.

APPENDIX

Earnings of Families Employed by W. G. and J. Strutt

(The positions held by each worker reveal a

TABLE

The Allsop

		1801				1802			
		1	2	3	4	1	2	3	4
		s. d.	s. d.	s. d.	s. d.	s. d.	s. d.	s. d.	s. d.
Thomas	Spinner . . .	134 0	205 3	192 6	127 9	181 0	205 9	174 9	
	Overtime . . .	23 10	23 2	15 0	24 10	24 0	25 0	24 0	
	Out workman . .								195 0
Thomas	Reeler					5 9	50 6	60 3	64 0
	Carder	36 9	41 0	44 0	42 0	32 9			
Samuel	Spinner . . .	65 6	68 6	70 3	9 3				
	Reeler				61 6	72 3	79 9	71 3	77 6
Sarah	Spinner . . .	69 0	76 0	87 0	85 9	72 9	69 3	85 3	86 6
Elizabeth	Spinner . . .	95 9	95 6	100 0	31 6	0 6			
	Reeler				27 3	84 9	92 3	92 3	80 0
Mary	Spinner . . .	86 0	89 6	78 0	88 9	13 3	1 0	1 0	
	Reeler					66 0	83 3	83 3	88 0
Ann	Picker	5 3	5 0	2 3			19 6		16 7½
	Spinner . . .			12 9	26 3			2 0	3 6
	Mill labourer . .								
Mean Weekly Earnings . . .		39 8	46 5	46 3	40 4	42 6	48 2	45 8	47 0

¹ Contributed by Dr. R. S. Fitton.

D¹

AT BELPER AND MILFORD, DERBYSHIRE, 1801–1805
considerable degree of mobility inside the mills)

D/I

FAMILY

1803				1804				1805	
1	2	3	4	1	2	3	4	1	2
s. d.	s. d.	s. d.	s. d.	s. d.	s. d.	s. d.	s. d.	s. d.	s. d.
195 0	195 0	147 6	195 0	195 0	195 0	195 0	195 0	195 0	195 0
60 0 0 6	63 0	63 2½	67 10½	70 4½	76 8½	84 11	90 9½	99 6½	83 2½
67 3	79 6	73 5	81 3	85 3	86 0½	81 7½	79 10	85 1	88 6½
85 9	95 6	103 5	107 4	120 3	120 8½	119 6½	113 5	107 2½	124 3½
87 3	95 3	90 6½	103 10	102 2½	87 9	91 11½	89 2	89 2	83 2
71 0									
	48 0	65 1½	69 2½	52 11	88 5	26 8½			67 4½
	1 0								
43 7	44 5	41 9	48 0	48 2	50 4	46 2	43 8	44 4	49 4

TABLE

THE BOND

		1801				1802			
		1	2	3	4	1	2	3	4
		s. d.	s. d.	s. d.	s. d.	s. d.	s. d.	s. d.	s. d.
George	Carder	152 0	158 0	189 9	180 3	178 6	182 0	206 0	210 6
	Overtime	13 0	12 8	12 6	12 10	12 8	12 2	12 8	12 8
John	Spinner	78 0	42 0	29 3	44 6	47 9	56 6	57 0	57 9
	Carder			14 9	13 6				
	Winder				3 9				
Edward	Spinner		17 0	25 0	26 3	23 9	24 9	25 3	25 0
	Carder	9 0							
	Reeler								
Robert	Carder	37 0	18 0	49 6					
	Winder					2 0			
	Spinner						44 9	38 0	38 3
Hannah	Carder	45 9	42 3	50 3	50 6	50 6	52 3	49 6	67 6
Eliza	Carder	53 9	52 6	57 3	11 6				
	Reeler				43 6	52 6	56 9	60 6	60 6
George, jnr.	Not stated								
Mary	Picker			37 6	36 0		11 3		
Mean Weekly Earnings		29 11	26 4	35 10	32 6	28 3	33 11	34 6	36 4

D/II
FAMILY

1803				1804				1805	
1	2	3	4	1	2	3	4	1	2
s. d.	s. d.	s. d.	s. d.	s. d.	s. d.	s. d.	s. d.	s. d.	s. d.
196 6	181 6	190 10½	214 2	220 1½	203 4	212 3	201 7	193 4½	192 1
11 11	12 6	12 10	12 8	12 8	12 6	13 0	12 10	12 8	12 8
56 6	71 0	77 1½	81 1	100 6½	95 2	68 6½	74 2½	82 6	83 4
						0 5½			
34 3	39 9	38 4½	41 3	40 6	41 10½	43 4	44 3½	49 4	53 10
		3 0							
1 0									
41 9	47 3	47 11½	49 2½	52 3	54 3	61 4	58 6	56 5½	56 5
90 6	103 3	109 6½	107 6	108 1	106 6½	106 11	101 3½	104 8	93 9
						54 1½	93 7½	99 2½	99 1½
70 0	71 0	65 5	55 7	8 1		7 7			
								26 4	16 2½
				29 8					
38 8	40 6	41 11	43 2	44 0	39 6	43 8	45 1	48 1	46 9

		1801				1802			
		1	2	3	4	1	2	3	4
		s. d.	s. d.	s. d.	s. d.	s. d.	s. d.	s. d.	s. d.
John, snr.	Carder	59 6	51 9	15 6	13 6	13 3	9 3	4 3	4 6
	Reeler								3 3
	Mill labourer . .	47 6	19 0	112 9	110 9	109 3	18 6	129 0	130 3
John, jnr.	Carder	53 0	67 6	68 3	53 9	46 9		64 9	71 3
	Spinner . . .					2 6			2 0
Mary	Spinner . . .	76 6	82 6	67 3	83 9	80 6	83 9	91 0	91 3
Jane	Spinner . . .	69 9	80 9	91 3	90 6	87 9	90 0	97 0	95 9
	Reeler								
	Picker	0 6							
Hannah	Spinner . . .	18 9	19 0	29 0	32 6	30 3	31 9	45 0	39 9
	Carder								
Susannah	Winder			0 5	16 3	22 6	22 0	24 6	28 3
	Picker								
	Mill labourer . .								
Charles	Carder	115 6	97 9	3 9					
	Spinner . . .		2 9						
	Mill labourer . .			117 9	116 6	69 9			
	Not stated . . .								
Mary	Picker	42 0	51 6	84 6	89 6	83 0	74 3	89 9	97 6
Eliza	Picker			1 0	19 6	42 3	22 6	4 6	
	Winder					0 9			
	Mill labourer . .								
Mean Weekly Earnings . . .		37 2	36 4	45 6	48 2	45 3	27 1	42 3	43 4

D/III

FAMILY

	1803				1804				1805	
1	2	3	4	1	2	3	4	1	2
s. d.	s. d.	s. d.	s. d.	s. d.	s. d.	s. d.	s. d.	s. d.	s. d.
2 3	20 3	0 5½							
	0 6								
137 9	117 6	83 10½							
101 5	107 6	101 11½	79 4	126 8½	127 11½	127 4½	128 1½	132 10	124 6½
90 9	69 0	0 4		13 10		1 3½			
	26 9	88 7	63 7	81 11½	88 3	92 10	100 6½	99 8½	97 0½
45 3	43 0	54 11½	48 1½	48 9½	48 2½	44 3	48 0	52 3	51 0
					2 4				
27 9	27 0	32 7½	28 5½	27 7½	32 4½	32 7	30 6½	30 4½	33 3½
	0 6					0 7½			
								5 9	
									37 8
54 5	81 9								
31 3	60 3	42 2	22 9		43 3	43 4	61 11	64 0	28 3
	0 6								
37 9	42 8	31 2	18 8	23 0	26 4	26 4	28 5	29 7	28 7

G

		1801								1802							
		1		2		3		4		1		2		3		4	
		s.	d.	s.	d.	s.	d.	s.	d.	s.	d.	s.	d.	s.	d.	s.	d.
Isaac, snr.	Spinner . . .	109	6	99	2	95	0	76	3	34	6	113	3	114	0	116	9
	Picker	1	9	0	6												
	Reeler																
	Carder			3	0	3	3										
	Mill labourer . .																
	In/Out workman .																
	Overtime . . .																
	Not stated . . .															20	3
Isaac, jnr.	Spinner . . .	80	0	84	6	56	9	75	3	82	6	68	9	97	6	90	9
	Reeler																
	Mill labourer . .											6	0				
	Not stated . . .															11	3
James	Spinner . . .	59	3	64	9	68	0	55	3	61	3	68	3	72	3	79	6
Millicent	Spinner . . .	68	9	66	3	75	9	58	3	80	6	86	6	85	6	87	0
	Reeler																
	Picker																
Hannah	Spinner . . .	76	9	88	0	24	9	71	9	76	3	83	9	96	6	119	0
	Picker					9	1½										
Mary	Picker	85	3	90	6	91	3	85	9	91	9	75	0	91	3	90	0
Richard	Carder																
Jane	Picker																
Mean Weekly Earnings . . .		37	0	38	2	32	7	32	6	32	10	38	7	42	10	47	3

D/IV

Family

	1803				1804				1805	
	1	2	3	4	1	2	3	4	1	2
	s. d.	s. d.	s. d.	s. d.	s. d.	s. d.	s. d.	s. d.	s. d.	s. d.
	21 6	120 0	48 6			63 5½	127 3½	125 0	126 11½	125 11
	5 0									
	76 9	6 0	54 2	140 0	88 7½					
		3 3			0 9½	1 8				
			18 4		44 9	35 8				
			7 0	12 6	6 4			12 8	25 10	25 4
	36 0									
	93 6	114 0	102 2	99 2	117 2½	115 1	71 2			
	85 3	89 9	89 8	90 5	89 11	94 11½	94 2½	104 2½	104 11½	98 2
	84 6	71 9	109 5½	111 8	107 8½	111 5	108 10½	104 11½	114 8½	96 8
		3 1½								4 9½
	110 6	64 3	86 9½	107 8	68 9	83 7	73 5	96 2½	126 7	119 8
	94 0	97 3	94 10½	102 4	64 6	70 2	78 0½	85 9½	71 0	78 5½
	43 9	52 0								
									34 1	40 1
	50 1	47 10	47 0	51 1	45 3	44 4	42 6	40 8	46 6	45 4

		1801				1802			
		1	2	3	4	1	2	3	4
		s. d.	s. d.	s. d.	s. d.	s. d.	s. d.	s. d.	s. d.
James	Reeler	128 0	184 0	162 3	153 6	159 9	154 3	149 0	144 9
Robert	Spinner . . .	32 3	43 0	45 6	23 6	34 6	9 3	47 0	56 0
	Reeler					6 0	17 3		
	Mill labourer . .					16 3			
Hannah	Spinner . . .	24 9	63 3	69 3	49 6	52 9	79 9	81 3	79 3
	Picker			1 3					
Ann	Spinner . . .	95 9	112 0	102 6	49 0	95 3	97 9	93 0	97 9
	Reeler								
Eliza	Winder	8 6	19 3	21 6	17 6	15 3	24 0	26 9	30 3
	Picker								
Sarah	Picker	57 6	76 6	54 0	22 9	50 9	76 0	63 0	18 9
	Spinner . . .					31 3	5 3	5 6	2 9
	Carder								57 3
	Reeler								
Mary	Reeler							36 9	62 6
Mean Weekly Earnings . . .		26 8	38 4	35 1	24 3	35 6	35 8	38 8	42 3

D/V

FAMILY

| | 1803 | | | | 1804 | | | | 1805 | |
| | 1 | 2 | 3 | 4 | 1 | 2 | 3 | 4 | 1 | 2 |
	s. d.	s. d.	s. d.	s. d.	s. d.	s. d.	s. d.	s. d.	s. d.	s. d.
	32 6	157 9	151 7	155 5	153 0	139 4	160 5	176 2½	170 3½	179 6½
	61 0	63 3	64 1	60 10	65 0	63 4	69 11½	71 11½	73 2	9 10
	77 6	57 9	81 8½	83 11	81 8	87 11	85 5	80 5½	88 9	88 7½
		0 3	0 6							
	98 3	56 9	48 3½	87 1½	91 7	93 10	91 3½	96 6½	96 3	98 8½
		31 0	34 5½							
	27 0	22 9	32 1½	30 6	32 10½	31 7	31 7	30 11½	29 9½	30 7½
		3 3								
		53 9	43 3½							
							3 8			
	57 9									
		9 0								
	69 0	76 0	73 5	80 1½	80 0	84 7½	75 10	86 6	81 5½	84 3½
	32 6	40 11	40 9	38 4	38 9	38 6	39 10	41 9	41 6	37 10

		1801				1802			
		1	2	3	4	1	2	3	4
		s. d.	s. d.	s. d.	s. d.	s. d.	s. d.	s. d.	s. d.
Joshua	Reeler							18 9	24 0
Ann	Carder			33 6	61 0	62 6	66 3	76 0	78 6
	Reeler								
	Picker			3 0					
Mary	Spinner . . .						7 3	31 9	33 0
	Picker								
George	Carder						13 3	0 9	
	Reeler							47 3	58 3
Alice	Winder								
	Picker								
Mean Weekly Earnings . . .				2 10	4 8	4 10	6 8	13 5	14 11

D/VI

FAMILY

	1803				1804				1805	
	1	2	3	4	1	2	3	4	1	2
	s. d.	s. d.	s. d.	s. d.	s. d.	s. d.	s. d.	s. d.	s. d.	s. d.
	24 9	31 9	30 2	32 1	32 0½	38 0	37 10½	36 1½	38 7	38 9
	76 9	75 3	45 8							
			33 3½	74 1½	69 5	111 9	104 9½	88 2½	74 2½	77 2½
		1 6						1 6		
	39 0	48 9	50 6½	59 9½	63 1	76 3	74 5½	83 4	73 4	76 10
		0 3	0 4							
	63 0	63 0	63 5	67 9½	69 9½	77 8½	86 5	93 9	95 5½	86 10
			2 11½	16 7	29 1½	31 0½	31 2	32 7½	33 6½	35 1½
										0 10
	15 8	17 0	17 5	19 3	20 3	25 9	25 9	25 10	24 3	24 3

		1801				1802			
		1	2	3	4	1	2	3	4
		s. d.	s. d.	s. d.	s. d.	s. d.	s. d.	s. d.	s. d.
James	Carder	38 3	35 9	60 0	58 3	42 6	66 0	75 6	73 6
Joseph	Carder	75 6	50 0	81 6	82 3	74 3	81 9	85 0	90 0
	Spinner . . .								
	Reeler								
Eliza	Winder	37 9	24 3	48 9	45 3	39 6	30 6	18 6	9 9
	Spinner . . .							20 0	27 9
Sarah	Picker	32 9	9 6						
	Winder						11 9	21 9	17 6
Mary	Spinner . . .	43 8							
	Winder		3 3	18 3	28 0	27 6	30 6	34 0	33 0
	Reeler								
Hannah	Winder			13 3	24 9	22 0	26 6	26 3	30 3
	Picker								
John	Spinner . . .		44 6	84 6		86 6			
Mean Weekly Earnings . . .		17 6	12 10	23 7	18 4	22 6	19 0	21 7	21 8

D/VII

FAMILY

1803				1804				1805	
1	2	3	4	1	2	3	4	1	2
s. d.	s. d.	s. d.	s. d.	s. d.	s. d.	s. d.	s. d.	s. d.	s. d.
85 0	83 6	112 8	112 6	108 4	91 5	88 8	89 9½	86 4	92 2½
99 9	94 3	107 8	62 10½	1 10½	12 0	10 6	4 6		
			61 9	124 3½	91 1	27 6	133 10	146 0	18 0
					11 3	76 0			
2 3									
44 9	46 9	81 7	86 1½	83 7	86 3	79 3½	81 10½	81 4½	81 8½
		1 8							
23 0	29 3	36 1	32 4½	32 9½	37 2	38 0½	37 7	33 9½	37 0
				17 5½	31 1	45 4			
29 3	44 3	38 11	29 9	16 10½	1 11½		61 2	59 0½	59 4
	6 6					0 11			
33 3	38 6	36 9½	38 2	40 6	43 2	44 3½	40 5	43 5½	45 3
		2 1½					1 2		
24 5	26 5	32 1	32 7	32 9	31 2	31 7	34 8	34 7	25 8

TABLE

The Tomison

		1801				1802			
		1	2	3	4	1	2	3	4
		s. d.	s. d.	s. d.	s. d.	s. d.	s. d.	s. d.	s. d.
William	Clerk	156 0	156 0	156 0	156 0	156 0	156 0	156 0	156 0
Mary	Reeler	108 3	117 0	109 0	103 6	53 0	105 3	103 9	102 3
Martha	Reeler		9 0	60 0	69 9	67 7	80 0	83 9	89 9
Alice	Carder		37 9	53 0	37 9	25 0	24 6		
	Reeler							51 9	62 0
Millicent	Reeler						64 3	25 3	56 9
Mean Weekly Earnings . . .		20 4	24 7	29 1	28 3	23 2	33 1	32 4	35 11

D/VIII

FAMILY

	1803				1804				1805	
1	2	3	4	1	2	3	4	1	2
s. d.	s. d.	s. d.	s. d.	s. d.	s. d.	s. d.	s. d.	s. d.	s. d.
156 0	156 0	156 0	156 0	156 0	156 0	156 0	156 0	156 0	156 0
97 0	107 0	103 $8\frac{1}{2}$	106 $0\frac{1}{2}$	94 $11\frac{1}{2}$	99 9	101 $1\frac{1}{2}$	98 11	61 $11\frac{1}{2}$	100 0
81 6	86 0	78 3	97 $3\frac{1}{2}$	85 $8\frac{1}{2}$	44 3	80 3	99 $4\frac{1}{2}$	67 $1\frac{1}{2}$	87 $8\frac{1}{2}$
67 9	56 9	69 $0\frac{1}{2}$	78 7	77 11	71 $10\frac{1}{2}$	82 $3\frac{1}{2}$	79 4	73 5	108 $7\frac{1}{2}$
19 6	55 9	77 $7\frac{1}{2}$	84 0	46 8			82 1	84 $5\frac{1}{2}$	56 $0\frac{1}{2}$
32 5	35 6	37 3	40 2	35 6	28 7	32 3	39 8	34 1	31 1

APPENDIX E[1]

DISTRIBUTION OF WINDERS', SPINNERS' AND REELERS' WAGES
1801–1804

TABLE E/I

DISTRIBUTION OF WINDERS' EARNINGS BY DATE AND SEX
AT STRUTT'S BELPER AND MILFORD MILLS

Up to	Weeks Commencing 1801				1802				1803				1804			
	January 2		July 3		January 1		July 2		January 7		July 1		January 6		July 6	
s. d.	M.	F.	M.	F.	M.	F.	M.	F.	M.	F.	M.	F.	M.	F.	M.	F.
0 6				1		1	1	1		1				2		1
1 0	2	4	1	4	1	6	1	2	1	1			1	1	1	
1 6	3	2	2	12	4	18	2	6	3	5	1	3	4	3	2	3
2 0	2	10	2	9	2	17	1	13	5	13	2	6	4	8	3	6
2 6	3	4	4	3		17	1	8	1	22		12	1	13	4	14
3 0		23	2	10		2	1	13	1	7	3	11	6	16	2	15
3 6	1	4	1	5		2		10	1	8	3	9	1	5	4	8
4 0		4		12			1	9		7	1	8		3		3
4 6				3		2		3		1		4				
5 0		1		2		3		4								
5 6		2										1				
6 0				1				1		1						
6 6														1		3
7 0				5				1		4						1
7 6								4				3		2		1
8 0												2		2		
Total	11	54	12	67	7	68	8	75	12	70	10	59	17	56	16	55

[1] Contributed by Dr. R S. Fitton.

TABLE E/II

DISTRIBUTION OF SPINNERS' EARNINGS BY DATE AND SEX AT STRUTT'S BELPER AND MILFORD MILLS

Up to	Weeks Commencing															
	1801				1802				1803				1804			
	January 2		July 3		January 1		July 2		January 7		July 1		January 6		July 6	
s. d.	M.	F.	M.	F.	M.	F.	M.	F.	M.	F.	M.	F.	M.	F.	M.	F.
0 6						1			2			1				1
1 0			2			2		1	1	4						1
1 6			2	1	5	4	2	3	2	1	1	1		1	1	2
2 0	2	1	2	1	1	2	1		4	5	2		3	5	2	2
2 6	2	1		2		2	7	3	1	5		3	3	5	5	2
3 0	3	4			4	6	3	3	1	4	1	4		2	1	3
3 6	1	3		1	3	5				4	5	6	2	7	4	
4 0	2	2	3	1	3	6	2		6	8	4	3	2	10	2	
4 6	5	3	2	3	5	16	4	3	4	7	3	5	2	7		8
5 0	1	3		3		13	1	4	7	7	1	5	5	11	2	10
5 6		9	2	1				5	2	11	4	8	2	9	1	8
6 0	2	11	2	3			5	3	2	11	2	3		9	3	10
6 6	1	7	1	4	1			11	2	13	2	16	4	13	5	9
7 0			3	2		1		9	2	25	2	16	1	20	1	20
7 6	1			2	1		2	14	1	15	3	22	1	16	2	23
8 0	1		1	14			2	12	1	7		9		10		19
8 6				10				2				8	4	7	4	10
9 0	1		1	4				2		1	1	5	1	2	1	4
9 6	1						2	1	1			3	1	1	3	
10 0			1						1	1	1		1			
10 6				1	2		2		2		3					1
11 0				1	1		2		1			2	3		1	
11 6									3		1		2		1	
12 0			1													1
12 6								1				1		1		3
13 0						1		1	1			1				1
13 6								1				2				2
14 0	1											1				1
14 6			1						1							1
15 0	1															
15 6								1								
16 0									1							
16 6			2									2	1			
17 0			1										1		2	
Total	25	51	23	53	27	58	39	76	53	126	43	120	40	136	49	133

TABLE E/III

Distribution of Reelers' Earnings by Age and Sex at Strutt's Belper and Milford Mills

Up to	Weeks Commencing															
	1801				1802				1803				1804			
	January 2		July 3		January 1		July 2		January 7		July 1		January 6		July 6	
s. d.	M.	F.	M.	F.	M.	F.	M.	F.	M.	F.	M.	F.	M.	F.	M.	F.
0 6		1	1			1				1		1		1		
1 0		2	1	4	1	2	1	1		2	3	3		2		
1 6		8	1		2	16		2		4		2	1	7	2	
2 0	3	8	1	9	8	18	1	6	2	9		2	1	3	1	
2 6	1	8	2	5	1	13	1	3	1	8		5	1	4	1	5
3 0	2	14		8	3	10	2	9	5	7	1	2	2	3		3
3 6	2	7	3	4	7	16	4	14	5	9	1	3	1	5	1	6
4 0	6	6	2	10	7	22	4	8	5	10	2	12	2	12	2	18
4 6	9	17		11	6	24	2	9	3	4	1	10	2	6	2	8
5 0	4	20		5	2	8	2	4	2	13		1	1	2	2	2
5 6	3	19	4	1	1	1	3	8	2	13	2	5	2	1	1	1
6 0	4	5	4	14	5	1	2	10	3	19		4	1	11	1	5
6 6	4	6	5	10	5	1	2	12	3	8	1	5	1	7		4
7 0			2	11				19	3	6	1	14	2	11	5	13
7 6		1	4	17	3		1	20	1	12	3	12	3	8	2	12
8 0	3		2	7			2	5	3	2	2	11	2	12	3	19
8 6	4		2	8	1		2	2	2	1		12	2	8	2	4
9 0	2	1	3	2				4	3	1	3	6	2	5		7
9 6	1						6	1	1			1	2	8		4
10 0		1	1		1		1	1	1		3	4	1	2	1	3
10 6			3	1	1		2		1		2	3	6	3	5	7
11 0			3				1		3		5	3	4		3	3
11 6			1						3		1	1	1		1	
12 0	1			1			2		1		2	2	1	1	1	3
12 6			3								1	3	1	1	3	
13 0							2				1		1		3	
13 6								1	2				1		1	
14 0							1		1		1					
14 6			1				1		1		2		1		1	1
15 0											2		1			
15 6							1				1					
16 0					1		1		1		1					
16 6																
17 0																
17 6																
18 0							1	1								
18 6			1										1			
19 0			1										1			
Total	49	124	51	128	55	134	54	140	58	131	42	127	48	123	44	128

INDEX